# PRIMAL

## POWER, STATUS, AND SEX IN HUMANS AND OTHER ANIMALS

## PAUL FELDMANN

COPYRIGHT © 2023 PAUL FELDMANN
*All rights reserved.*

PRIMAL
*Power, Status, and Sex in Humans and Other Animals*

ISBN  979-8-218-30274-0  *Paperback*
       979-8-218-30275-7  *Ebook*

*Collages by* Alexis de Chaunac

MAMMUT AMERICANUM PUBLISHING

*This book is dedicated to my father.*

# CONTENTS

Introduction   ix

## PART I. SENSUAL EXPERIENCES

1. Rock, Paper, Scissors   3
2. The Sound Of Alpha   19
3. A Rose By Any Other Name   37

## PART II. KINGS AND QUEENS

4. Alpha Icons   61
5. Primate Politics and Alphas   77
6. It's Good to Be the Queen   95

## PART III. LOVE AND WAR

7. Morituri Te Salutant   123
8. A Call To Arms   139
9. Sneaky Fuckers   155

## PART IV. GENDER MATTERS

10. Polygyny   173
11. Alpha Inversions   189
12. Noblesse Oblige   205

Conclusion   227
Notes   237
Additional References   245

# INTRODUCTION

"What makes us people and not computers is emotion. We have little grasp of our true nature, of what it is to be human and therefore where our descendants might someday wish we had directed Spaceship Earth. Our troubles, as Vercors said in You Shall Know Them, *arise from the fact that we do not know what we are and cannot agree on what we want to be. The primary cause of this intellectual failure is ignorance of our origins. We did not arrive on this planet as aliens. Humanity is part of nature, a species that evolved among other species. The more closely we identify ourselves with the rest of life, the more quickly we will be able to discover the sources of human sensibility and acquire the knowledge on which an enduring ethic, a sense of preferred direction, can be built."*

—EDWARD O. WILSON

## THE BOY AND THE NATURAL WORLD

Since I was a little boy, I've been fascinated by nature: from backyard bugs to birds, fish, small mammals, and even, to a certain extent, humans. At a young age, I did not comprehend much about human nature, but I was intrigued nonetheless. I was trying to make sense of the world, and while I enjoyed exploring and observing the natural world without humans, I still lived in a world dominated by them. When I was around other people, those dynamics interested me, and though I wouldn't have called it this yet, my interest in humans at that time was limited to hierarchies, power, and status—and, much later, sex.

I grew up as a shy introvert, and I often retreated within and had self-doubt. I felt confident in sports but not much else. I spent long periods of time alone, climbing trees and exploring the backyard, looking for insects and other organisms. I had a profound curiosity about the natural world. I felt at peace in nature and playing sports. Growing up as a shy and quiet kid I would observe the world around me. That's when my fascination with nature and hierarchies began to grow. When you are quiet and alone frequently you have plenty of time for introspection.

I am still a curious person. I still enjoy the process of learning, and in many ways, the contents of this book have been bouncing around my head, in some form or another, since I was that little kid. As an adult, my love of nature remains strong. My desire to better understand power, status, hierarchies, and sex in humans is also at the forefront of my mind; however, biology is complicated, and various elements frequently interact to influence how the world develops. The simple answers I once sought are no longer realistic or reasonable.

I began to recognize the dichotomy between the formal, scientific experience of nature and the raw, wondrous presence of nature itself, and I quickly reconciled these two grand impulses in my education. As an undergraduate, I studied raptor migration and songbirds. After earning a Bachelor of Arts in environmental studies and origins of behavior, I embarked on a rigorous program of fieldwork with the Smithsonian Institution. I worked alongside researchers in Ecuador to establish a long-term project to monitor rain forest dynamics.

After my time in Ecuador, I began my graduate studies. I worked in the field in both Bolivia and Puerto Rico, where I collected data for my master's thesis on the influence of hurricanes on the Luquillo Experimental Forest. More recently, I conducted fieldwork on the island of Madagascar, the coast of South Africa, and the Gulf of Tadjoura in Djibouti. I also created a program for National Geographic Television.

My thirst for learning more about organisms and ecosystems of the world has kept me moving and has fueled my passion for over forty years.

We are such a social species, and power, status, sex, and hierarchy structures change, at times with great rapidity. Human social structures are fluid, flexible, chooseable, and changeable. But what about the natural world? What can we as humans learn from other species regarding hierarchies, power, status, and sex?

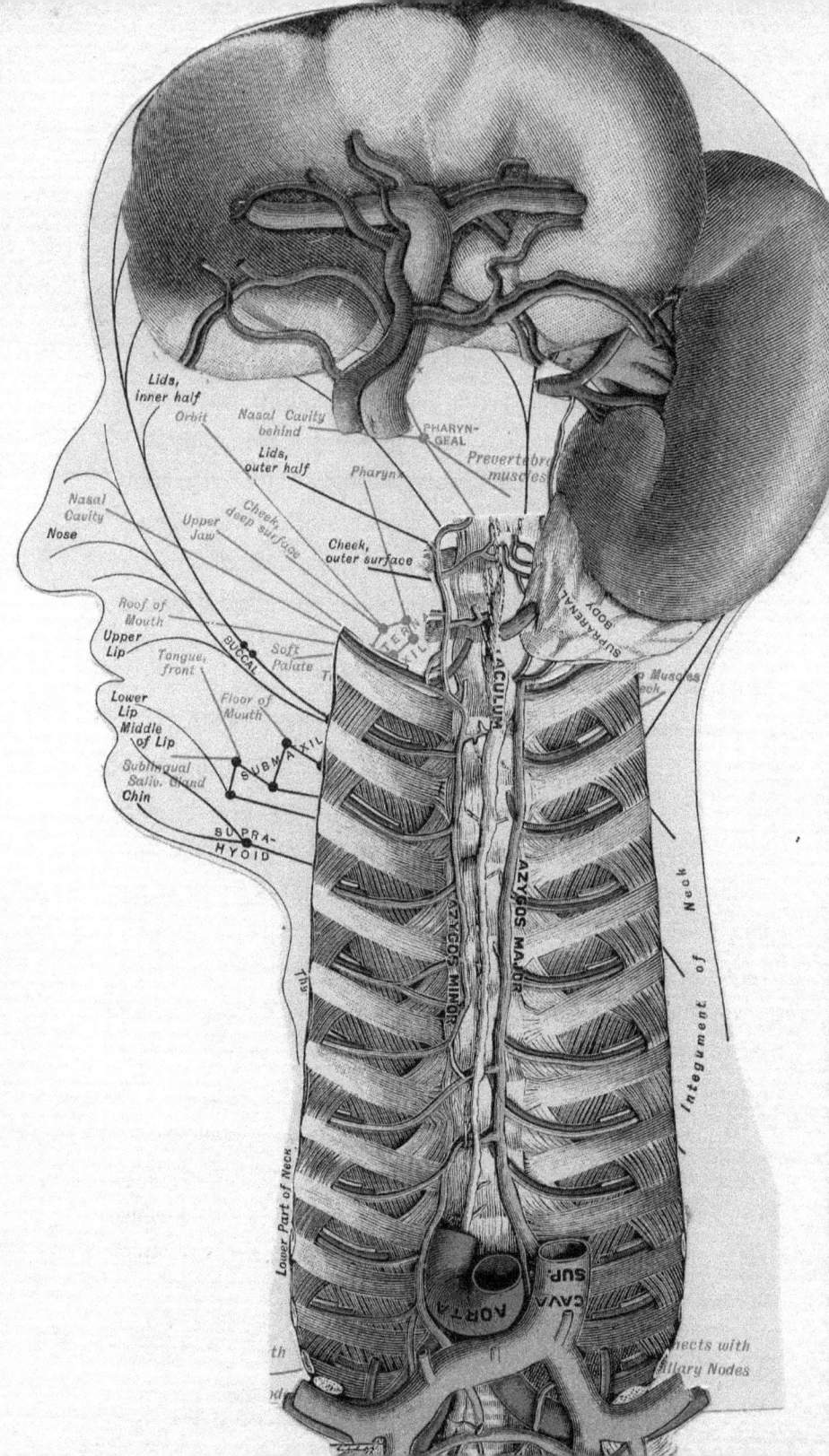

We will explore that question throughout this book, looking at a wide breadth of disparate strategies and structures, such as sound and smell in organisms as varied as crickets and muskoxen. We will go across the globe, from the depths of the ocean to the Mongolian steppes. We will find that the natural world tells us so much and provides such beautiful, varied, and vibrant forms of information. Yes, there may be some anthropomorphizing, but not in a way that undermines the science or possible insights into our own human nature. This book represents the fascination of that young boy who loved the natural world but lived in our very human, very complex, and very social world. They speak to one another in curious ways. This book is about that conversation.

## THE MASCULINE STRATEGIST

I think that we as humans are walking contradictions, myself included. There is often a duality to the way we think, feel, process, interpret, and act. We are messy, messy creatures, not easy to define or understand. As the brilliant biologist Edward O. Wilson said, "We have Stone Age emotions, medieval institutions and godlike technology." We are a complicated species, especially when it comes to hierarchies, power, sex, and status.

Through this book, I discuss quite a few strategies from a masculine perspective. I don't think that being masculine is toxic, though I think it is tragically real that toxic specimens see themselves as some form of alpha example of the masculine. I struggle to isolate those from one another. Certainly, some of the common traits associated with toxic masculinity (mental and physical toughness, aggression, self-sufficiency, and stoicism) can be repugnant in extreme doses, but they are not intrinsically malignant. Even aggression can be channeled properly. I generally think that those traits deemed as toxic have potential benefits to men—but as ever, in context.

If we consider the distinctly familiar common ground between species—with social strata of dominance from alpha to beta to the omega at the bottom—we must also note that these hierarchies are not entirely static and that individuals will often slide up or down the ranks as opportunities arise. Indeed, few species include males that do not attempt to assert their dominance when given a viable opportunity to do so.

Therein lies the key to our confusion. The concept is an unerringly mobile one. Strategies vary widely across species, and many species (including humans) use more wildly subtle, eloquent, bizarre, and beautiful methods both to display and maintain social status.

Alpha males in many species use an incredible array of behaviors to assert their alpha status: a soothing posture, fluid dance, warbled song, vivid coloration, repugnant scent, or nuanced bellow. These nonaggressive, nonviolent methods are often meant to create and sustain the alpha status in a metacommunicative collection of declarations.

As I was writing this book, people often asked me what it was about. I usually answered in the most general of terms, but on one particular occasion, I mentioned dominance hierarchies. This set the conversation down an interesting path. The guy I was speaking to got very excited because he fancied himself as a dominant individual.

I get it. Many men I've met desire, both consciously and subconsciously, to be in positions of power in social hierarchies. This guy may or may not have been in a position of power, but in his mind he clearly thought that he was a dominant individual. And how ironic that men who frequently trumpet their dominance are also quite frequently the antithesis of dominant or are perhaps in a position of power in only one small sliver of their lives.

Why are men so attuned to dominance and power? One notable answer from the animal kingdom would suggest it is because it can lead to more mating opportunities and greater access to resources.

And perhaps that shows us how difficult the concept is to tackle. Masculinity is challenging to define because different nations, religions, and social classes have varied ideas about what it means to be a man. Humans are very tribal; we are influenced by family, friends, religion, sex, culture, and country. Anthropocentrism reigns supreme. It is hard for us to unhitch ourselves from emotion and use our critical thinking and reason to evaluate subjects that are now deemed problematic or controversial. But that, in part, is the project of this book. I hope to look at the complexity of mating structures and strategies, the wonder of hierarchies in the natural world, to suggest that there are no easy answers. I'd like to get comfortable with that uncomfortable notion.

## THE BOOK

Are there a specific set of traits that an alpha has, such as hard-driving competitiveness, interpersonal impatience and difficulty controlling anger? Must one have a monomaniacal obsession to achieve a high-ranking status? Some hierarchies are essential to the existence of the organization—the military, some corporations, some governments, some communities, and some families, for example. Social hierarchies also exist in prisons, law firms, and sports teams.

Why are hierarchies necessary, and do alpha males always sit atop these hierarchies?

Everyone walking this planet has questioned their place in society. From as far back as I can remember, I wanted to be a garbage man and a naturalist. Back in my childhood, we used to have steel garbage cans that had to be lifted and carried some distance to the garbage truck. This was strenuous, hard, heavy work. My father's work was also physically and mentally taxing. He repaired printing presses with massive gears, rollers, gripper bars, and cylinders. It was not uncommon to see people in the industry with missing digits. Though I was too young to understand social hierarchies at the time, to me, these jobs embodied what it was to be a man.

We must not overlook science, specifically biology, simply because it doesn't fit within a particular narrative. We might take shallow comfort in knowing that we are not alone.

Hierarchies are not something unique to a country or culture. They are not even unique to humans. They are a global phenomenon in which many organisms participate. Alpha males and females perch atop the social hierarchies of a remarkable variety of species: insects, fish, birds, and the vast majority of mammals. As such, an intense level of scholarly attention has been focused on the accurate description of this fundamental social dynamic, yet we remain curiously empty-handed when we try to shape a viable, unifying criteria for the "alpha-ness" of the alpha. Even more so with the human being, we are left rather puzzled by the form and function of the alpha male.

Well. We most certainly shall see. Each chapter will look at these wild, strange, and compelling species to help tell an unexpected story of our human condition. Please join me as we delve headlong into this wondrous world.

Chapter 1 explores what the game of rock, paper, scissors can teach us about the theory of evolution. We can find reproductive variations in this classic children's game distributed across such varied species as lizards, marine isopods, humans (of course), and Gouldian finches. But why? What do these species tell us about the delicate balances and counterbalances of physical form and mating strategies? First, we should observe the way that these competing, and sometimes leveling, strategies potentially disrupt the classical notion of "alpha" and "fittest." For every rock, there is a paper. And so on.

Chapter 2 is all about acoustics. We will sing a song of fitness, physical form, and even fighting ability. That's precisely what we humans do (often subliminally) when we measure social interactions from the height or depth of vocal range. Bison, field crickets, and greater white-lined bats also use sound to broadcast a breadth of information about themselves. Their insights offer us a chance to think in quite a different way about what we do with our voices.

Chapter 3 sniffs out pheromonal communication. The animal examples in this chapter include the aptly named muskoxen, brown lemmings, and mice. All of these species (and humans) use pheromones to communicate, with massive implications on their social behavior and reproduction. Specifically, we will look at how females use pheromones to choose mates. Female members of a species may select particular males depending on their array of pheromones as well as behaviors and other characteristics, a choice that further complicates our understanding of how exactly selection operates.

Chapter 4 pauses for a moment to examine three historical human figures, each of whom sat atop their human hierarchy. Mongol leader Genghis Khan created the largest land empire in history. Moulay Ismail Ibn Sharif, Sultan of Morocco, amassed an empire with massive armies. Emperor Charlemagne controlled most of Western Europe. All three of these men had a huge empire and large armies, and they were all prolific progenitors. As a result, they left gigantic genetic legacies. What can these individuals teach us about how the forces of dominance and power worked throughout human history?

Chapter 5 will delve into the surprisingly dynamic world of primate politics by examining rhesus macaques, savanna baboons, and chimpanzees. All three of these primate species have extraordinarily complex social systems. We will also become acquainted with shrewd political strategists from human history: Xunzi, Kautilya, and Machiavelli. What can we learn from them and our primate brethren that can help us navigate politics and our current social structures?

Chapter 6 pivots from all the testosterone and focuses instead on females of the species. The female pipefish reverses what some might consider traditional sex roles, with males caring for the fertilized eggs in their specialized brood pouch. Moreover, female pipefish have sexual ornaments, and they usually initiate sexual behavior. Spotted hyenas continue to challenge our understanding of social hierarchies in mammals in that the females possess a pseudo-penis and are the highest-ranking members of the social hierarchy, while males reside at the bottom of the social structure. Honeybees are also a female-dominant species; the queen and the worker bees, all of whom are female, perform all the tasks within the colony. Females across all species show incredible variation when it comes to power, status, sex, and hierarchy.

Chapter 7 enters the "arena"...as it relates to humans, marine iguanas, and birds such as the greater prairie chicken and the sharp-tailed grouse, that is. In this chapter, we'll learn about the ways in which we are drawn to arenas in order to witness the spectacle, to behold the gladiatorial spirit in action, but also to observe the importance of competition both for the competitors and for the audience. There is much more at play here than we might initially presume. The audience of the arena reflects the subtle way in which we observe one another's behavior, competitive spirit, and dynamism, and the way that behavior shapes our choices as both males and females of the species.

Chapter 8 picks up the theme of physical confrontation as violence dominates the contest. The human male body has evolved to fight (most often) against other males, and usually with a brutally

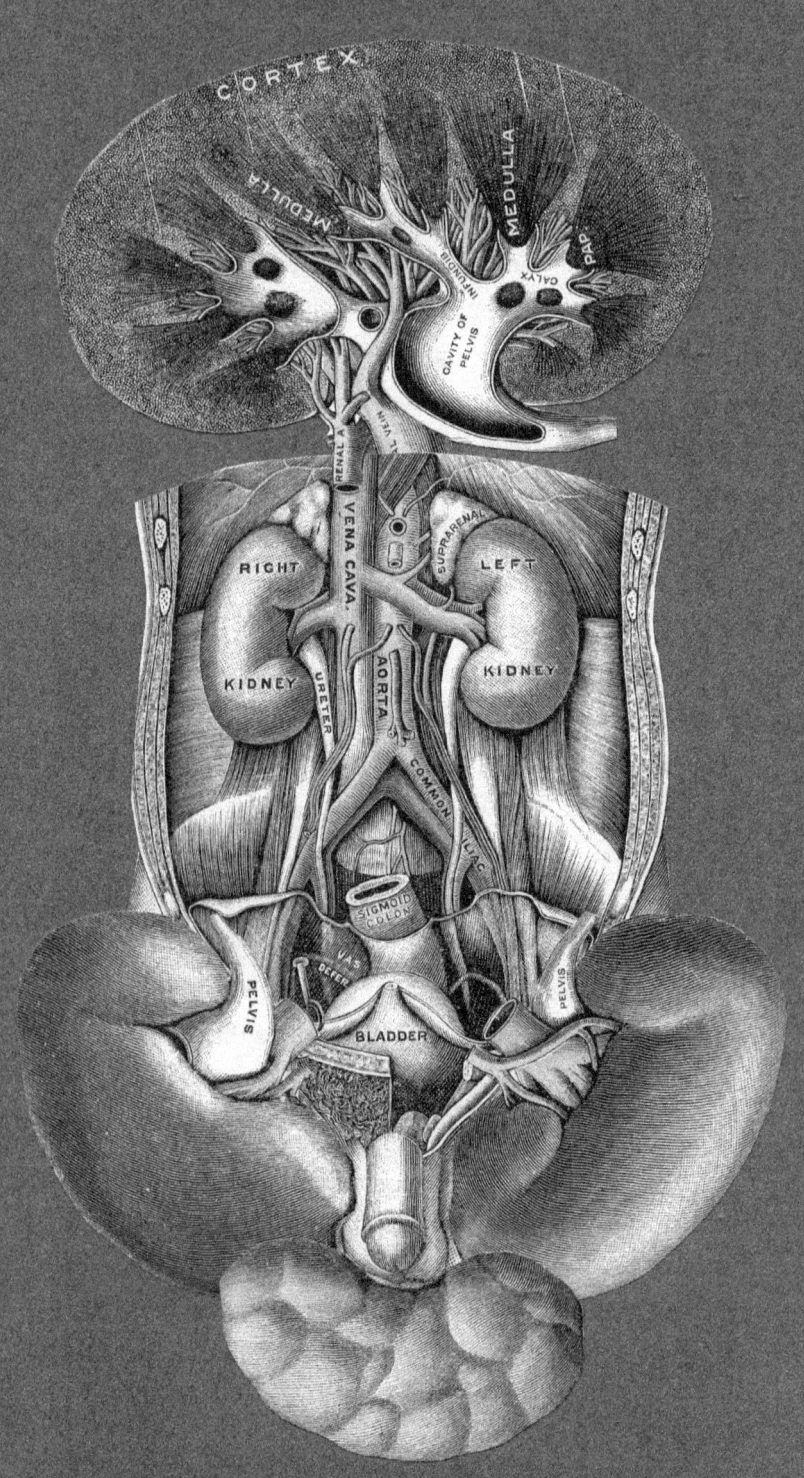

convenient tool: the fist. Other species as wildly varied as bighorn sheep, rusty crayfish, and horned beetles fight for access to females through physical combat using horns and claws—tools evolved for this specific purpose. Males across species fight in wondrous and terrible ways, but how fascinating that the evolutionary process anticipates and shapes such a variety of species for this purpose.

Chapter 9 explores the lives of animals that have also found alternative ways to be successful without fighting, such as octopuses, bluegills, and red deer. Low-status males of these species may try more sneaky methods of mating if they have little opportunity of reaching females through traditional channels like fighting or signaling of their prowess. What might be the benefits for "sneaker" males amongst humans? If a male is smaller in stature, and/or otherwise weaker, he benefits from this opportunistic approach. Sneaker males may even do better than average, conventional males in terms of reproductive success.

Chapter 10 tackles the subject of polygyny. Horses exhibit a polygynous mating system similar to that of lions and elephant seals. Of course, there is still an honest brutality to be found in these species: as with many male mammals, they fight with other males over access to an assemblage of reproductive females. Hierarchy influences reproductive status and reproductive success; alpha males control access to optimal resources, and those resources feed the nature of one's alpha status. In conjunction, females and their offspring get priority access to resources.

Chapter 11 explores the wondrous complexity inherent both in the natural world and within our own extraordinary species.

Indeed, there are an endless number of ways in which organisms can reproduce and even change sex. We will learn that with the blue-headed wrasse, a female can become a male when the dominant male is removed. The female's behavior is the first thing to change, and she becomes more aggressive and starts to perform male courtship behaviors—very soon afterward the ovaries transform into testes. We will also learn about the peculiar practice of penis fencing in flatworms and the odd foreplay of love darts in garden snails.

Chapter 12 turns the lens on what many people would consider the archetypical, king-of-the-mountain types of species: gorillas, gray wolves, and elephants. All of these examples represent wonderfully majestic animals—noble, even. However, more than merely their individual impressive stature, these animals are an inspiration when we consider the way in which they work through the complex mechanisms of their social structure.

# PART I
# SENSUAL EXPERIENCES

# ONE
# ROCK, PAPER, SCISSORS

"And now let me collect my strength and my thoughts and focus with everything I have on the horror of our earthly existence, on the imperfection of the world, on the myriad lives torn asunder, on the beasts that devour one another, on the snake that bites a stag as it grazes in the shade, on the wolves that slaughter sheep, on the mantises that consume their males, on the bees that die once they sting, on the mothers who labor to bring us into the world, on the blind kittens children toss into rivers, on the terror of the fish in the whale's entrails and the terror of the beaching whale, on the sadness of an elephant dying of old age, on the butterfly's fleeting joy, on the deceptive beauty of the flower, on the fleeting illusion of a lovers' embrace, on the horror of spilt seed, on the impotence of the *aging tiger, on the rotting of teeth in the mouth, on the myriad dead leaves lining the forest floor, on the fear of the fledgling when its mother pushes it out of the nest, on the infernal torture of the worm baking in the sun as if roasting in living fire, on the anguish of a lovers' parting, on the horror known by lepers, on the hideous metamorphoses of women's breasts, on wounds, on the pain of the blind..."*

—DANILO KIS

## REMBRANDT

Touch is thought to be the most developed sense that humans possess at birth, while vision is the least developed.

In Leiden, in the 1600s, a Dutch teenager painted his interpretation of the five senses. These five oil paintings were painted on small wood panels and include *A Pedlar Selling Spectacles (Allegory of Sight)*, *Three Singers (Allegory of Hearing)*, *Unconscious Patient (Allegory of Smell)*, *Stone Operation (Allegory of Touch)*, and *Allegory of Taste*, the last of which is lost. This artist, who was acutely aware of the importance of the senses, especially the visual/sight, was Rembrandt.

Rembrandt's interpretation of the sense of sight, *A Pedlar Selling Spectacles*, portrays an elderly couple buying a very specific type of glasses: a pair of pince-nez spectacles. Pince-nez glasses lack temples and temple tips to support them on the ears; they are solely supported by pinching the bridge of the nose. The young

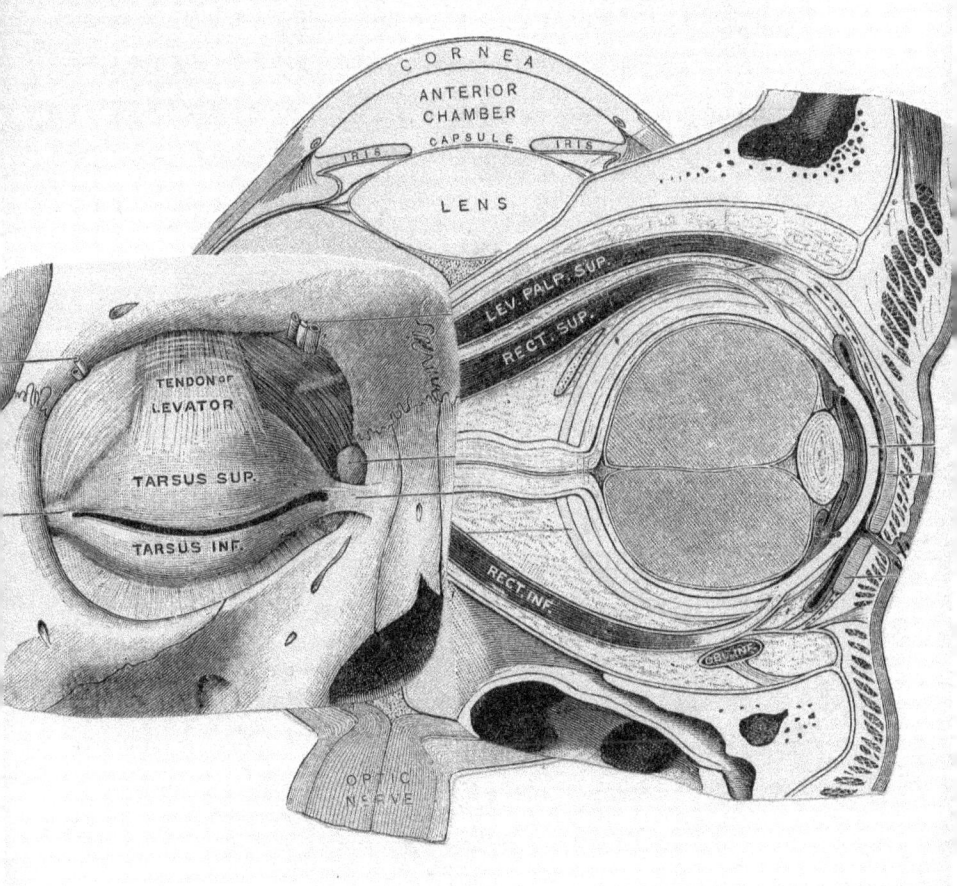

Rembrandt may have been depicting a peddler taking advantage of an elderly couple whose vision was too compromised for glasses, highlighting the importance of sight in avoiding being cheated.

In the animal world, especially among mammals, visual acuity is paramount in mate selection and hierarchy formation. Scientists at the University of Western Australia showed that men were able to judge the faithfulness of a woman by looking at a photograph of that woman's face.[1] Previous studies have shown the same of women who looked at photographs of men's faces.[2] Both sexes seem to have some ability, through their sense of sight, to weed out possible unfaithful partners, which over evolutionary time seems to be a useful skill to have. A study by Schmitt and Buss found that 60 percent of men tried to poach a woman for a brief sexual tryst while 31 percent of women admit to being successfully poached from their committed relationship for an extra-pair copulation.[3] Just as the young Rembrandt knew, our vision is paramount in avoiding betrayal.

Unlike Rembrandt, who never ventured beyond his own country, I was fortunate enough to travel with my family to Holland when I was a teenager in the late 1980s. My father, who was raised in Holland, moved frequently during the war, and we visited some of the homes where he had lived. We traveled through Zeeland, visited the North Sea, and spent an evening in the town of Middelburg, where we stayed at a small hotel that offered a complimentary breakfast. I woke up ravenous and hit the breakfast offerings hard. After having eggs, bread, cheese, and yogurt, I decided to have some cereal for a kind of breakfast dessert. The cereal came in little boxes, and I must have plowed through ten or twelve of them. As a matter of fact, I ate all of the cereal that they had. I was a teenager, and it was imperative to meet the needs of a growing body. When my grandfather saw the row of empty cereal boxes in front of me, he wanted to leave the hotel as quickly as possible before the hotel discovered how much food I had eaten.

Hundreds of years prior to my visit, Rembrandt was a teenager in the town of Leiden, which sits in the province of South Holland, directly to the north of Zeeland. The coat of arms for Zeeland depicts a lion with its lower half submerged under water with the Latin text *Luctor et emergo*, which means "I struggle and emerge." This phrase might be in reference to the low elevation of the country on the whole. The Netherlands literally means "lower countries." A good portion of the country sits below sea level. A nation struggles and emerges from the sea while two teenagers centuries apart struggle and emerge from adolescence.

## ROCHAMBEAU

We can all remember a time during our childhood, standing on the wood chips in the playground, playing the game of rock, paper, scissors to solve a problem such as who got to go first picking teams. It was often a best-of-three scenario. Rock, paper, scissors is also called "roshambo," the zero-sum game, or the hand game. The game is usually played with two people using their hands to create the three objects: rock, paper, or scissors. The rock, closed fist, beats scissors, represented by the index and forefinger. Scissors beat paper, flat, palm-down hand. Paper beats rock. This is how the three game elements interact. It is played throughout the world and has survived for hundreds of years because it is egalitarian and fair. Adults can learn a lot from this children's game.

The game rock, paper, scissors originated in China in the 1600s. It was then imported to Japan in the 1700s. As the Japanese traveled to Europe in the twentieth century, they brought rock, paper, scissors with them. The game spread through Europe and eventually made its way to the United States in the 1930s. Some of you may know the game as Rochambeau (or roshambo), possibly named after the French nobleman Comte de Rochambeau, a leader of French troops who fought against the British during the Revolutionary War. His name was used as a code word during the war, but that does not explain the connection to the game of rock, paper, scissors.

Children (and adults, on occasion) use the game to solve problems. Back in 2005, Takashi Hashiyama, president of a Japanese electronics corporation, could not decide between Sotheby's and Christie's to auction off some of the company's art collection, which included works by Cezanne, van Gogh, Gauguin, and other greats and was worth an estimated $20 million. Christie's won the game with scissors.

## SIDE-BLOTCHED LIZARDS

Humans are not the only ones that play the rock, paper, scissors game. Side-blotched lizards (*Uta stansburiana*) also play the game, so to speak. Side-blotched lizards are common in western North

American deserts. They are small lizards, averaging about five inches in length, with a light gray and tan coloration. These lizards also have a black blotch, hence the name, behind their front limbs. Males are generally larger than females, and during the breeding season males exhibit orange, blue, or yellow throats. This is where the rock, paper, scissors game comes into play.

Side-blotched lizards are polymorphic. Breaking the word down, we know that *poly* means two or more and *morph* means forms. During breeding season, males exhibit three different throat colors, each representing a different mating strategy. One morph of the male lizard wins over another but not over the third; no single mating strategy prevails.

Orange-throated males are extremely aggressive and control large territories, with more females in these areas. They are heavier than the blue- and yellow-throated males and also have higher levels of testosterone. Blue-throated males are not as dominant and defend smaller areas, but they excel at guarding the females that are within their territory. Yellow-throated males are not at all aggressive and do not have any territory. Instead, they mimic females in both coloration and behavior, thus fooling the orange- and blue-throated males. These yellow-throated males slip into the territories of orange-throated males and fertilize females of the unsuspecting dominant males. It is interesting to note that if a dominant male dies, the yellow throated male changes into a blue-throated male and maintains the territory.

Dr. Barry Sinervo was the first to document the three-morph mating system in side-blotched lizards: "As in the game where paper beats rock, scissors beat paper, and rock beats scissors, the wide-ranging 'ultradominant' strategy of orange males is defeated by the 'sneaker' strategy of yellow males, which is in turn defeated by the mate-guarding strategy of blue males; the orange strategy defeats the blue strategy to complete the dynamic cycle."[4]

## MARINE ISOPODS

Another species that exhibits three male morphs is the marine isopod *Paracerceis sculpta*. Marine isopods look like an aquatic version of pillbugs (or roly polies, as we called them when we were kids). Marine isopods are invertebrate crustaceans, a group of animals that includes shrimp and crabs. They are small organisms, reaching a length of only one centimeter, and are found in the shallow waters of the intertidal zone, living among seaweed, sponges and barnacles.

Marine isopods are native to the Pacific coast of North America, but similar to the rock, paper, scissors game, they have been introduced to many parts of the world, including China, Europe, and Australia. Akin to the side-blotched lizards, marine isopods also employ an interesting mating strategy during the breeding season.

Male marine isopods are also polymorphic, existing in an alpha, beta, and gamma form. They reproduce in sponges. Alpha males are the largest and maintain and defend a harem of females within the sponge. Marine isopod beta males employ a similar tactic to that of the yellow-throated side-blotched lizard males. Beta males look like females and mimic female behavior. This allows them to invade the alphas' territories undetected. The gamma form is the smallest and mimics the juvenile form. These qualities afford the gamma male the ability to slip into the alpha male harems and mate with the females. Instead of investing in size and fighting ability, gamma males invest more energy into sperm production. Beta males have invested an intermediate amount of energy on sperm production and alpha males have invested the least amount of energy into the production of sperm. As with the side-blotched lizards, the marine isopod morphs all use different strategies to achieve reproductive opportunities.

## GOULDIAN FINCHES

Another rock, paper, scissors game occurs in the Gouldian finch (*Erythrura gouldiae*), a beautifully colored bird native to Australia. Male dominance hierarchies exist in the Gouldian finch based on color polymorphisms. These finches exhibit three distinct naturally occurring phenotypes: yellow-headed, red-headed and black-headed.

The red-headed Gouldian finches are the alphas in this triad of polymorphs, with the submissive yellow-headed males at the bottom of the hierarchy and black-headed males at an intermediate level of dominance status. Australian scientists Donald C. Franklin and P.L. Dostine stated, "Although black-headed males are not socially dominant, they are the most common head morph in wild populations (70%), while red-headed males are moderately common (30%) and yellow-headed males extremely rare (estimated at one in 3000–5000)."[5]

Given that red-headed males are favored by females, one would think that they would predominate in wild populations, however they are not the most common morph. This illustrates that the advantages of being at the top of the hierarchy are counterbalanced by higher levels of the stress hormone cortisol. This is a case of the advantages being canceled out by the concurrent disadvantages of being a red-headed male, hence the lower numbers in the wild.

## HUMAN SOMATOTYPES

Humans also engage in a form of rock, paper, scissors when it comes to mating strategies. Human males and females are critically attuned to somatotypes (body types) across countries and cultures. There are generally three body types in humans: endomorphic (someone who is heavier and rounder with higher body fat and less muscle mass), mesomorphic (an individual with a muscular build but not bodybuilder size), and ectomorphic (someone who has a lean, slender body with slight muscular development).

A study was conducted across New Zealand, the United States, Cameroon, and China to determine if females preferred a certain body type.[6] In this study, a fourth body type was added: average (somewhere in between the mesomorphs and the endomorphs in terms of fat and muscle). Females looked at images of these body types and rated them for attractiveness. In this study, females overwhelmingly picked the mesomorphic and average body types. Evolutionarily, this makes sense because these traits may indicate health and fitness and at one time were necessary for fighting, hunting, protection, and survival.

What body type do men prefer in women? A cross-cultural study showed that males generally prefer females with a hip-to-waist ratio between 0.6 and 0.7.[7] In this study, men were shown back-posed images with hip-to-waist ratios ranging from 0.5 to 1.0. Body types with a healthy distribution of fat may be a signal of health and reproductive potential.

Humans are a sexually dimorphic species, which means that males and females exhibit different characteristics beyond the most obvious difference in sexual organs. Two differences that most people notice most often are height and weight: men are, on average, heavier and taller than females.

Humans are acutely in tune with the heights of others. I can remember times in grammar school when we were lined up by height. We tend to classify one another in one of three groupings: tall, average, or short. Given the tremendous variation that we find both within and between human populations, it seems odd that height continues to be something that humans are aware of.

Studies have shown that females prefer males who are taller than they are.[8] What is interesting is that women want taller men more than men want shorter women. One study found that "women are most satisfied when their partner was 21 cm taller, whereas men are most satisfied when they were 8 cm taller than their partner."[9] Why do women prefer taller men? Taller men are perceived as more dominant than shorter men. Taller men often have positions of leadership and have higher overall incomes. Taller men have greater reproductive success, although one study, by a group of Dutch scientists, showed that average-height men (in this study the average height was 5'9") had greater reproductive success over taller men.[10] They used data from the Wisconsin Longitudinal Study which included around 3,500 men. They speculate that average-height men had better reproductive outcomes by marrying earlier, possibly as a result of a longer reproductive window.

As with side-blotched lizards and marine isopods, multiple morphs exist in humans, each with varying degrees of reproductive success. Rock, paper, scissors is an apt analogy in regard to mate selection, the only difference being that not every strategy is equal. One strategy may outweigh the others for periods of time but eventually gets supplanted. If we go back to height in human males, females find taller men more attractive during the fertile phase of their cycle. As professor Alan F. Dixson stated, "Indeed, sexual selection is likely to have favored female preferences for taller partners who were more successful in these new kinds of inter-male competition, hunting and survival skills."[11]

This is interesting in that it does not seem to translate into greater reproductive success for taller men. Females are primarily selecting taller men for extra-pair copulations or short-term relationships.[12] Average-height men married at a younger age and were more successful at finding a mate versus taller and shorter men. Scientist Gert Stulp stated, "The number of children born to a male is only a proxy for fitness, which should ultimately be measured far into the future." There could be many unknown correlated factors that are involved in both height and reproductive success.

## HEPHAESTUS

Ever since our ancestors left the forest for the savannas and became bipedal organisms, our vision has been paramount for our survival. As humans, we are constantly assessing the physical characteristics of our fellow humans. Even in mythology, the gods assess physical characteristics.

Of all of the ancient Greek gods, only one was physically ugly and lame. His name was Hephaestus. Hephaestus was the eldest son of Zeus and Hera. Hera was so upset at having an ugly child that she flung him off Mount Olympus and into the sea, breaking his legs in the process. He was raised by Thetis instead of Hera.

Hephaestus had none of the physical characteristics of the other gods but was a physically strong blacksmith who created great works of beauty. Hephaestus was the god of fire and forge, the only god who worked. Think about that: the god who was considered malformed, crippled, and lame outworked all the other gods. And in spite of his physical appearance, his wife was Aphrodite, the most beautiful of all the gods. How did this happen?

Hephaestus devised a plan to exact revenge on his mother: he made a golden throne and sent it to her. When Hera sat on the throne, it trapped her in it, and only Hephaestus could free her. Zeus offered two things to Hephaestus to free Hera: the first was a seat among Olympians as the god of forge, and the second was the arranged marriage to Aphrodite. Hephaestus was happy with this resolution and freed his mother. Zeus was also happy because Hera was free, and the compromise with Hephaestus also solved the problem of the constant fighting among gods and mortals over the beautiful Aphrodite.

## DAVID AND GOLIATH

As we have seen with marine isopods and humans, size matters. One of the most famous stories in human history deals with size: the story of David and Goliath. Goliath was a giant, armored-up warrior. David was a much smaller shepherd. The David and Goliath analogy is used frequently to describe corporations versus small businesses, sports teams, fights, and even so-called intellectual pedigrees.

In this story, the little guy actually had the advantage. David's speed, mobility, strategy, and skill (specifically slinging) allowed him to easily defeat the much larger opponent. David also took advantage of a medical condition that Goliath had. As Malcolm Gladwell stated, "He looks and sounds like someone suffering from what is called acromegaly—a disease caused by a benign tumor of the pituitary gland." This disease can also cause vision problems.

In other words, Goliath was a slow, lumbering, visually impaired giant. David should have been the favorite to win the battle.

Just as we have seen with the marine isopods, side-blotched lizards, Gouldian finches, and humans, there are many different morphs that all find varying degrees of success. Some morphs may be more successful than others, but the other morphs do not cease to exist; therefore, evolutionarily, they have been successful at transferring their genes to the next generation.

## CONCLUSION

Professors Barry Sinervo and Curtis Lively sum up this chapter nicely, stating, "The prevalence of multiple morphs is a challenge to evolutionary theory because a single strategy should prevail unless morphs have exactly equal fitness or a fitness advantage when rare."[13] But as we have seen in side-blotched lizards, marine isopods, humans, and Gouldian finches, multiple morphs exist, and all have varying degrees of success when it comes to mating. The rock, paper, scissors game has been incorporated into evolutionary game theory. The strategies used by the aforementioned species continue to be successful. Those lower-ranking males have found ways to compete with the alphas and still be successful.

What can we learn from these aforementioned animals? What do you do if you have a slight build or perhaps a bigger body type? You cannot change your bone structure, frame, or height; however you can change your fitness, musculature, appearance, confidence, posture, and strategy. Take control of the things in your life that you can change. Learn from the side-blotched lizards, and employ a different strategy. Turn your weakness into a strength. Remember that even the biggest, strongest man has weaknesses; he may just be better at hiding them than other people are.

We all doubt ourselves at points in our lives. This is part of the human experience. Humans are at times frail, weak, vulnerable creatures. People will doubt you, put you down, and look to exploit physical differences. Just remember that there are many ways to be successful. We will always battle our own fears and insecurities, but we can learn to lessen them or even master them. Our personal demons, which we all have, keep us stuck or even spiral us down.

So get out into nature. Nature heals. Hold yourself accountable for your actions, or lack thereof. Own your shit. Go for a run or walk. Lift weights. Or just wake up earlier. I believe people are capable of making incredible changes in their lives.

Being an artist, Rembrandt understood the importance of his senses, especially that of sight. Rembrandt used his sense of sight to create works of art that have stood the test of time. Vision is one of the most important senses for humans, and we rely on it in part to help us choose both long-term and short-term partners. Humans rely on their vision to assess the fitness (or lack thereof) of potential mates and to spot potential infidelity and fertility. While looks aren't everything, they may hold the key to reproductive success or failure.

Most teenagers find that time of their life to be quite awkward, and I was no exception. It is an awkward time due in part to the profound changes that are occurring within the body. I liked the feeling of getting stronger. I started working out with weights for the first time in my teenage years. I, like most teenage boys, was a voracious eater. I wanted to get stronger and fill out my frame and the combination of eating a lot of food, working out, and going through puberty helped achieve those goals.

## TWO
# THE SOUND OF ALPHA

*"Dying cricket—
how full of
life, his song."*
—Basho

### SOUND

We can say with little hesitation that we are overwhelmingly an audio-visual species. We rely on these two senses more than any other sensory impression. And while humans are a bit of an anomaly in this sense (the majority of other organisms on the planet utilize a range of sensory organs in ways that we are just beginning to understand), we humans nevertheless rely almost exclusively on sight and sound, in that order.

In this chapter, we are going to investigate a sensory experience that is both significant and surprisingly sly at times. Specifically, we will begin to explore the sense of sound with a keen focus on its complicity in the creation of social hierarchies.

Sound can play a role in the fundamental properties of our identities. The process was slow and eventual, but I remember vividly several precise moments when my voice began to change from adolescence to young adulthood. These were small moments, of course, but they remain vivid and important to me. I remember overhearing a family friend observe the change in my voice with an offhand comment to my mother after a visit. Hearing the recognition from someone outside our immediate family felt like a dramatic shift in my sense of self—I was proud, embarrassed, shy, and excited all at once. And I remember answering the family phone we had mounted on the wall next to the kitchen and being caught flat to hear the seemingly sudden depth in my hello, as if the voice came from someone else. Who was this person speaking with some new version of my voice?

Though not nearly so dramatic as other changes in my body, here was a secondary sexual characteristic (one quite pronounced in the distinction between adolescence and adulthood, as well as between males and females) that announced this awkward but exciting time. This curious, unwitting break in my voice signaled with clarity that I was becoming a man.

Thousands of years of evolution have driven the difference in voice pitch among males and females, but what forces have driven this distinction? And why? Why should a notable majority of men register low vocal tones?

We can observe and measure some significant aspects of the phenomenon. Men report they do not desire to be with a female who has a deep voice, and conversely women do not fancy a male with a high-pitched voice.[14] Scientific teams led by researchers David A. Puts and David R. Feinberg have found that women perceive men with lower-pitched voices to be more attractive, stronger, more competent, and more trustworthy. Men perceive women with lower-pitched voices to be less attractive.[15] Beyond these perhaps standard sexual characteristics, when it comes to leadership, both men and women prefer male and female leaders who have lower-pitched voices.[16] This last part feels particularly compelling—that beyond sexual characteristics, we tend to associate qualities such as leadership and social hierarchy with the seemingly unrelated sound of one's voice.

And how fascinating that a fixation of this nature has woven its way into all manner of fundamental mythologies designed to express a core facet of the human condition.

## ADAM'S APPLE

Many people are familiar with the story of Adam and Eve. It is fundamental to the creation myth in each of the "big three" world religions: Judaism, Christianity, and Islam. It also includes a relatively small detail that loops seemingly unrelated concepts directly to the sound of the human male voice.

In the classic telling, Adam and Eve were the first man and woman from which all of humanity originated, such that every human would have descended from this single pair of people.

But here we are. In the telling, the Divinity created Adam, the first human, from the dust of the earth and placed him in the Garden of Eden. God then instructed Adam that he could eat freely from the garden, with the exception of a singular tree—the tree of knowledge of good and evil—for fear that on the day that Adam ate from that tree, he would surely die.

In time, God created Adam's new companion, Eve, and for some time, Adam and Eve lived pleasantly in the Garden of Eden. Then one day Eve came upon a cunning serpent who correctly pointed out that God had never instructed Eve not to eat from the tree and that they would not, in fact, die from eating the fruit. And so she was deceived into disobeying the spirit, if not the letter, of God's instruction.

The narrative suggests that God discovered their transgressions and banished them from the Garden of Eden. Calamity ensued. God cursed each of the principal characters: the serpent would forever crawl in the dirt, while Eve (and all future women) would suffer pain during childbirth. For his part in the original sin, Adam (and all future men) would labor for food instead of eating freely in the garden. God also made a chunk of the fruit, perhaps the forbidden apple, stick forever in Adam's throat, which was passed on to all future men with the moniker "Adam's apple" to mark humanity forever with the consequences of this sin.

How curious that this detail should emerge from a complex narrative tapestry about deception and shame. The Adam's apple, a

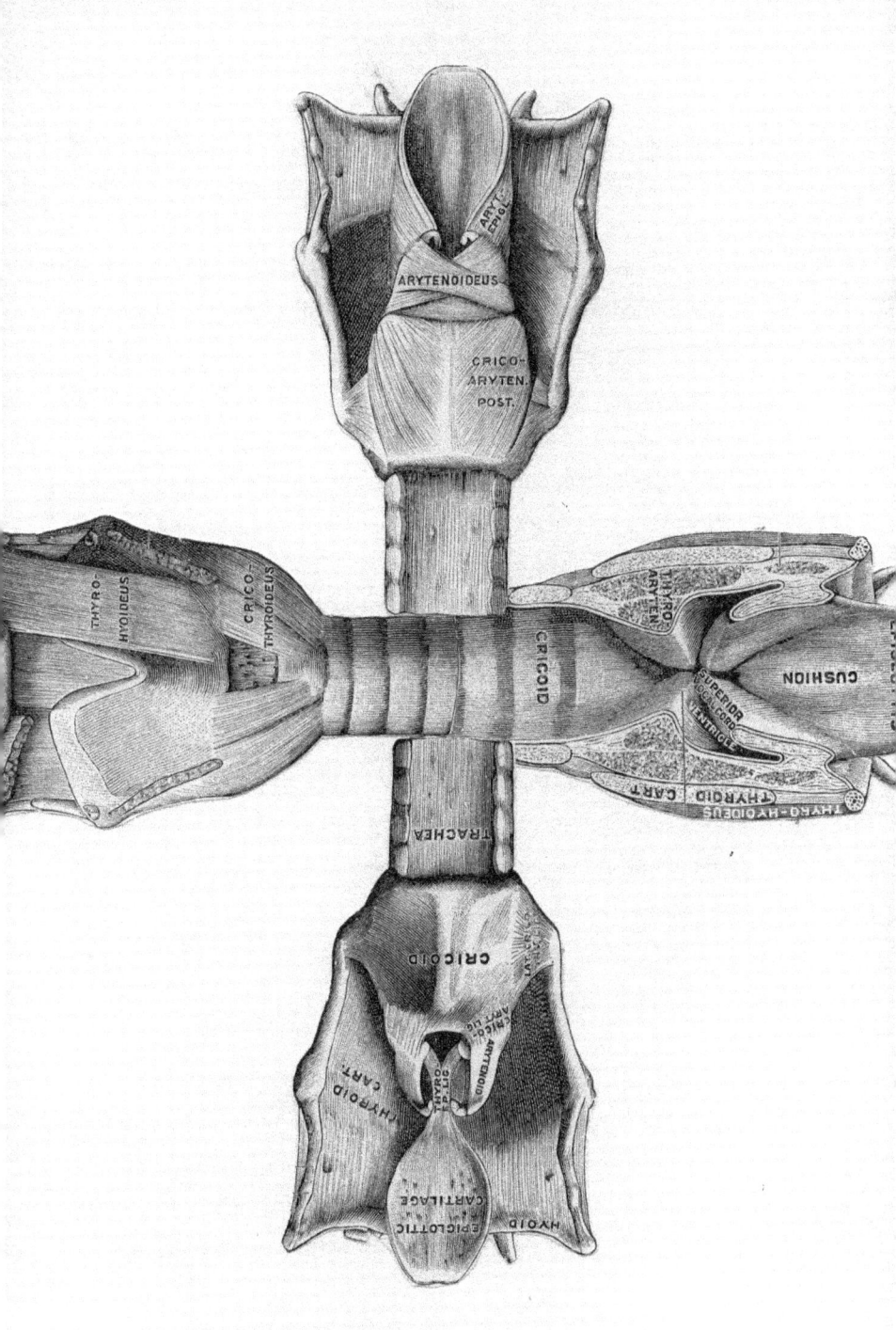

secondary sexual characteristic linked to the relatively deep sound of the male voice, seems a strange, almost arbitrary, consequence of sin.

The "Adam's apple," which has been present as an expression in English since at least 1625, is more technically known as a laryngeal protuberance, which is formed in the cartilage of the larynx, a hollow muscular organ that is involved in breathing, produces sound, and protects the trachea.

As with the deepening voice, the Adam's apple does not become noticeable until puberty, when it grows in both males and females. Although both sexes experience growth, it is more visibly significant in men. And with this we might observe that the larynx plays a key role in phonation. There are two sets of vocal cords within the larynx. When we want to make a sound, the vocal cords close, which forces air to pass over them, in turn creating vibrations culminating in the formation of sound. It is these same sounds that we will examine in this chapter. We will return to human-generated sounds in a moment, but first let's look at some of the ways non-human species communicate via sound.

## FIELD CRICKETS

The sound of a cricket is ubiquitous in summertime in the United States. For me, crickets and cicadas are two sounds that immediately resonate when I think of the soft summer months. Even in the urbanized areas of Chicago, the crickets and cicadas form a veritable wall of sound each year. And while the sounds we hear from these invisible hordes may all sound like one blended song, male crickets actually produce a variety of acoustic signals. Therein lies the beauty.

Male field crickets (*Acheta domesticus*) have a three-song repertoire. Their acoustic production consists of an aggressive chirp used when fighting among other males, a calling song used to attract females, and finally, a courtship song used directly prior to mating. The field cricket mating system consists of males competing over calling burrows, which act as the ideal real estate. Males call to attract females, and females select males based in part on their song. Once the female decides on a male, they typically touch each other's antennae, and a beautiful courtship song commences. Finally, mating occurs.

Scientist David Gray has studied house crickets in order to discern how female crickets process acoustic information. What type of information is the female house cricket gleaning from male chirps? His study demonstrated a relationship between the acoustic signals emitted by males to attract females and the size of the males being chosen by the females.[17] Female house crickets preferred the songs of large males. In the 1970s, another scientist, Owen S. Crankshaw, found that female crickets preferred the calling songs of dominant males.[18] Crankshaw reported that subordinate males called with a greater frequency but that dominant males had a "brighter" call. Smaller males may be more likely to employ an alternative mating strategy such as satellite behavior, which seizes opportunities with females that are drawn in by the calling abilities of the larger males.

Why do female house crickets prefer large male house crickets? Sexual selection would suggest that females are assessing males' genetic quality. Furthermore, according to Gray, if size is inherited, then selective females may have more fertile daughters and more aggressive and attractive sons. Gray's previous studies showed that large males were more symmetrical and lived longer, which means female house crickets are better off selecting males that chirp in a manner that signals their larger size.

## BISON

Bison (*Bison bison*) also use sound to communicate both their social quality and their physical condition. Millions of bison once ranged from Alaska all the way down to northern Mexico, but these majestic, iconic animals were nearly hunted to extinction. Now they are found primarily in the western portions of the United States and Canada on private and protected grasslands and open savannas. They are massive mammals (ranging from 770 to 1,900 pounds and six to twelve feet in length) with an unmistakable shoulder hump, giant head, and horns.

Bison are social animals and group with one another according to sex and age. Female groups consist of females, a few older males, and males under the age of three. Males over the age of three leave the herd and join bachelor herds or live alone. Bachelor herds and female herds come together during the breeding season.

During the rut, males maintain a harem of females, and the males "mate-guard" the females by chasing away and fighting rival males. During breeding season, fights are common among the males, as is wallowing, when bison roll around in the dry ground in a bowl-like depression. When bison wallow, they are giving themselves a dust bath, which can provide some relief from biting insects. During the breeding season, mature males urinate in the wallow prior to rolling in it, which acts as an advertisement to other males of their physical condition.

Tree horning is also a behavior that is thought to deter insects. Bison rub their horns against trees, specifically aromatic ones such as cedars and pines. The aroma or sap from the trees acts as an insect defense. Horning activity is higher during the summer months, but it is unclear if this is associated with the shedding of their winter coat, the rut, or insects.

Dominance hierarchies exist for both male and female bison. A male's dominance is related to its birth date, bellowing, and fighting ability. Bison born earlier in the breeding season have a distinct advantage in that they are generally larger and more dominant as adults and thus continue the cycle, breeding early in the rut.

Dr. Megan Wyman has spent years investigating acoustics across a variety of animal species, and she set out to measure the sound amplitude, or sound pressure levels, within bison groups. Wyman found that acoustic signals can encode and transmit a variety of biologically significant information, including species, sex, individual identification, age, size, physical condition, competitive aptitude, mate success, reproductive success, and mood. Her study showed that males increase call amplitude in response to female and rival male calls.[19] Males may use bellows to drive off challenging males and defend breeding territories. Bison bellows may be a sexually selected signal that females use when selecting a mate and also in male–male competition.

We know that alpha male bulls obtain significantly more copulations and have better reproductive success than lower-ranking males; likewise, mate-guarding, fighting, and bellowing are all energetically costly activities that confer a male's fitness if he is able to successfully do all of the aforementioned things and maintain his high rank in the hierarchy.

Wyman's findings showed a positive association between amplitude and physical condition but a negative association between amplitude and mating and reproductive success. This is counterintuitive because high-quality males can bear the costs of producing louder bellows.

Wyman states that "a plausible explanation for these quieter, high-quality bulls is that they do not need to 'shout to' rivals because their competitive ability (which rivals may use to assess the probability of winning in an escalated dominance interaction) is already evident either in the spectro-temporal parameters of the vocalization or in other sensory modalities such as visual or chemical displays." The spectrotemporal receptive field is a time-frequency measure of the auditory neuron's response. Further studies may reveal that bisons' bellow amplitude may be a sexually selected signal.

## GREATER WHITE-LINED BATS

Bats are primarily known for their echolocation abilities but far less so for their vocal displays. The greater white-lined bat (*Saccopteryx bilineata*), also called the greater sac-winged bat, is primarily found in tropical forests ranging from Mexico all the way down to Brazil, and many male bats use robust vocal displays. As the name suggests, the greater white-lined bat has dark fur with two white stripes running down its body and wing sacs. They are insectivores that use echolocation to find their prey.

In a similar manner to the bison we discussed above, greater white-lined bats also have social hierarchies in males and in females. Males defend harems, which usually consist of three to five females, from other males. Females are larger than males, so although males guard harems, females ultimately decide where their mating resources will be allocated.

Males use short territorial songs to ward off rival males and maintain and defend roosting and foraging territories in order to attract females. They also employ a variety of tactics to attract females, including olfactory, visual, and vocal displays.

One peculiar display that males use involves their wing sacs. Males spend a considerable amount of time cleaning their wing sacs with saliva and urine. Once the sacs are clean, the male will collect a genital secretion with his chin and apply it to the wing sacs. With this task complete, the male will perform his flight display, hovering over the female and flapping his sacs toward her. This behavior is called "salting" and is usually reserved for females from outside the harem. Females that are part of the harem receive a different type of courtship display. The male bats hover and perform a song that may continue on intermittently for an hour. If a female is receptive, she will swat at the male with her wing.

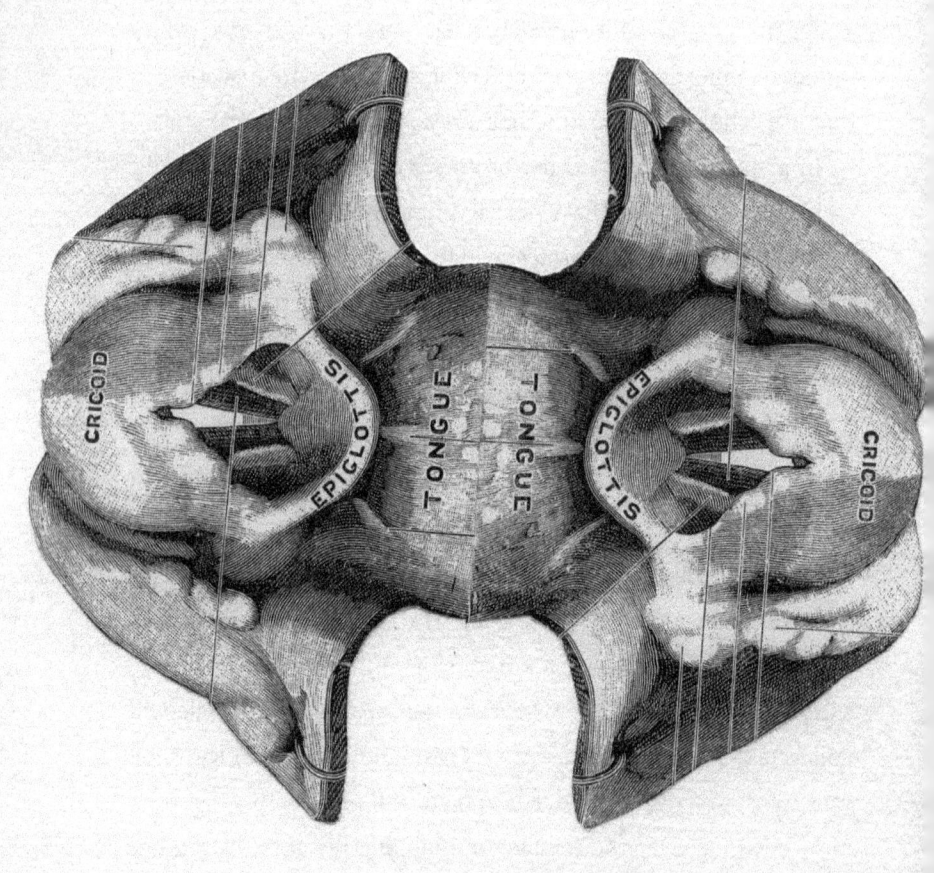

Males that produce more complex songs will generally have more females roosting in their territories. The larger the harem, the more reproductive success for the male bat. Hierarchy among males seems to be organized in part based on seniority. Female social hierarchies are determined by physical interactions, with the winning females taking the warmest area of the roost, highest from the ground. Studies by Christian Voight have found that 60 percent of females visit multiple harems per day. Another study suggests that female greater sac-winged bats assess the complexity and diversity of a male's vocal display and choose to mate with him.[20]

## HUMAN VOICE PITCH

As males enter puberty, the increase of androgens causes a growth of the vocal folds both in length and thickness. Males have vocal folds that are 60 percent longer than females' vocal folds. This causes the fundamental frequency of male voices to be lower. Voice pitch differentiation between males and females is considered to be a secondary trait used in sexual selection. Studies have shown that heterosexual females prefer the men's voices that are lower in pitch.

When women are in the fertile phase of their ovulatory cycle, they show a preference for males with lower-pitched voices and rate the voices for short term sexual relationships as opposed to long-term committed ones. The follicular phase is also known as the pre-ovulatory phase; it is the first half of the menstrual cycle that begins on the first day of the period and continues for ten to seventeen days. During this phase, women are known to select for height and scent. Women may exhibit this pattern of preferences in part because taller, leaner, more muscular males (visual cues), males with greater bilateral symmetry (olfactory cues), and males with low voice pitch (auditory) signal the possession of genes that increase immune system function. All of this clearly identifies that males and females are both selecting for better breeding material.

But sound works in peculiar and distinct ways here. Males with low-pitched voices are also associated with high testosterone and low cortisol levels. This combination has been previously linked to immunocompetence. Scientist David Andrew Puts has researched extensively with regard to sexual selection and human voice pitch. The results of one his studies indicate that "a masculine, low-pitch voice increases ratings of men's physical and social dominance, augmenting the former more than the latter; and men who believe they are physically dominant to their competitor lower their voice pitch when addressing him, whereas men who believe they are less dominant raise it."[21] So men with lower voices appear more dominant, and likewise dominant men also lower their voices in relation to one another in same-sex hierarchical interactions.

David Andrew Puts also determined that voice pitch increases mating success: men with a lower pitch reported more sexual partners. Puts and his colleagues suggested that low voice pitch evolved in men for two reasons: first, perception of physical dominance—low-pitched voices in men signal to other males, which in turn allows these dominant males to acquire more resources, which ultimately can lead to more mating opportunities; second, females associate low voice with good genetic fitness, which signals sexual attractiveness precisely when these females are most likely to become pregnant.[22]

A compelling study was conducted in Scotland that observed voice pitch in women as well as alterations to voice pitch when women spoke to men that they found attractive.[23] These (and other) studies demonstrated that men prefer a higher pitch in women's voices and that high voice pitch in females may indicate fertility. So just as females are assessing men's voices for mate quality, males appear to be doing the same with women's voices. Research suggests that high-pitched voices among females may confer information about a woman's reproductive health which often includes facial femininity and beauty, all of which men find attractive. Scientist Paul Fraccaro and collaborators designed a study in which women read a scripted message after being shown a masculinized prototype face and later on, separately shown a feminized prototype face. Women who had a preference for masculine men spoke with a higher voice pitch while women who preferred feminine men also spoke with a higher voice pitch. Women alter the pitch of their voice to men they find attractive: whether they prefer a masculine male face or a feminine male face makes no difference.[24]

Among the Hadza, an Indigenous group of hunter-gatherers living in Tanzania, men that have lower-pitched voices have, on average, more offspring.[25] Both men and women with attractive voices have more sexual partners, have sex earlier in life, and have more extra-pair copulations compared to individuals with voices rated as less attractive. Studies conducted in Europe and North America found that women prefer lower-pitched male voices.

Researchers have also determined that there seems to be a relationship between low fundamental frequency and large body shape in males. Fundamental frequency is simply the lowest frequency produced by any instrument. In this case, the instrument is one's voice.

Fundamental frequency is determined by the vibration of the vocal folds. Scientists Sarah Evans, Nick Neave, and Delia Wakelin discovered that a male's low vocal pitch can provide information about body shape and upper body musculature. Their study found that men with low fundamental frequencies had larger bodies, specifically with more muscle on their upper bodies.

It is interesting to note that although women prefer lower-pitched voices, there is a limit to the low end of the pitch. Women select for pitch above 96 Hz, which scientists suggest may be because extremely low pitch can indicate disease or damage caused by smoking or hyperpituitarism, among other problems.[26]

What we hear as we are speaking sounds drastically different to what we hear when our voice is played back. Like many people, I don't like to hear my own voice, and I remember people in school making fun of my voice because I tend to speak slowly and with deliberation.

I have also noticed that I modulate my voice depending on the setting and who I am speaking to. The fundamental frequency of an adult male is between 85 Hz and 180 Hz. The fundamental frequency of an adult female is 165 Hz to 255 Hz. I tested my voice on the voice analysis app called Vocular. These are my results: I had a voice depth of 93 Hz and an average of 117 Hz.

So much information can be gleaned from someone's voice. We can tell if someone is happy or sad, interested or uninterested, excited or scared, flirtatious or standoffish. Voice pitch is an overlooked auditory signal that perhaps subconsciously drives males and females during mate selection. Both one's speaking voice and one's singing voice provide relevant information about the individual producing the sound. Singing and speech are universally shared across human populations. The spoken word and singing are similar in that they both take a long time to learn through practice, and their production can be energetically costly, but there are some differences. Singing is more physically demanding because one must be better at controlling the air pressure in their respiratory system, have greater vocal control, and greater muscle activation to produce the sounds. A joint effort of scientists from Brazil and the Czech Republic found that "Attractiveness of both singing and speaking voice is perceived in a similar way and is connected to a higher pitch in women and a lower pitch in men."[27]

## CONCLUSION

Voice pitch is used in animal communication to convey authority and deference, maybe because low pitch heightens the appearance of size. It may not be surprising that voice tone affects mate attractiveness and same-sex rivalry, given this social function and potential links with immune function.

As we have seen with house crickets, bison, and greater white-lined bats, a male's song may contain information about his fitness, fighting ability, or physical condition. It is fair to say that we humans also recognize and process the height or depth of a voice in social interactions. While many animal species lower vocal pitch prior to an aggressive encounter, voice pitch in humans communicates a spectrum of information to the opposite sex. Perhaps unsurprisingly then, both human females and males also assess each other through acoustic signals.

# THREE
# A ROSE BY ANY OTHER NAME

"This is simply to inform you:
that the thickest line in the kink of my hand
smells like the feel of an old school desk,
the deep carved names worn sleek with sweat;
that beneath the spray of my expensive scent
my armpits sound a bass note strong
as the boom of a palm on a kettle drum;
that the wet flush of my fear is sharp
as the taste of an iron pipe, midwinter,
on a child's hot tongue; and that sometimes,

*in a breeze, the delicate hairs on the nape  
of my neck, just where you might bend  
your head, might hesitate and brush your lips,  
hold a scent frail and precise as a fleet  
of tiny origami ships, just setting out to sea."*

—**KATE CLANCHY**

## SMELL

We humans are largely visual creatures, and I suspect at times this leads us to disregard the potency of our other senses. Specifically here, I am thinking of the sense of smell (olfaction). Odor is a wondrous and strange power. Certainly, I am aware of the powerful way in which scent can trigger memory. I recall vividly the scent of the home where I grew up. Likewise, I think of times with a lover who would not wash a pillow when I was traveling so that my scent would linger in my absence. Parents often describe to me the powerful, intense emotional experience when they smell their infant children.

But this only touches the surface of what subtle scent can do between human beings—of the intense bond shared not just through memory and emotion of lovers, but also woven into the very composition of their love. We know that we can recognize the smell of our most intimate connections, but science suggests that scent plays a hand even in our choice of whom we create those intimate connections with in the first place.

## BOLIVIA

I recall where I was the moment that I heard Tito say the words, "*Un hombre debe oler a pólvora y tabaco.*" A man should smell of gunpowder and tobacco.

We were deep within the Beni Biosphere Reserve in northern Bolivia, where the rainforest subsides gently into the savanna and creates small islands of forest. Our re-censuring team of American, British, and Bolivian scientists had finished work for the day. The humidity was thick, almost stifling—and even more so beneath the jungle canopy, such that the dense air felt almost chewy in my mouth as we came around a thick copse and into something like a gentle clearing. Tito ambled up. He was a small man, but exceptionally large in personality. Tito was among the Bolivian support crew, and he had an unwavering familiarity with the forest and commitment to his work that was inspiring. Although not a scientist, Tito was knowledgeable about the forest in ways we could only aspire to be.

So when he spoke, in his manner, I listened.

Tito was laughing to himself as we started to unwind from the day. We were soaked through as much from the thick air as from the heat. There was no pretense or need to care about how bad we smelled.

Tito sat with his back along the slope and wiped his hands against his jeans. It was pointless—the earth in his fingernails was going to take more than that to get his hands clean—but he didn't really care anyway. He pulled the oily tobacco pouch from his pocket and skinned out a set of rolling papers, delicately balancing the first while he pulled a plug of tobacco and parceled it into the folder paper between his mud-stained fingers. A cigarette well earned after a day of rigorous toil.

I wasn't accustomed to seeing hand-rolled cigarettes or the raw pungency of the wet tobacco; it was oily in the air. He must have seen something on my face when he made that remark.

Tito's point hung like the smoke in the still air, made all the more vibrant as the sunshine pierced the canopy. What should a man smell like? It was a strange idea that I had never really considered before. Here in the jungle, this seemed utterly meaningless. There was no space or need for deodorant, and far less for any affectation of perfume or cologne. The very idea felt utterly absurd, oppressive.

And yet, nature provides us countless examples of the ways in which the animal world communicates volumes of information through these unseen gestures. Smell, even when we have not considered it, shapes far more of our world than we might otherwise imagine.

## ROMEO AND JULIET

If we jump across time and across the untrampled Bolivian landscape to Verona and its famous star-crossed lovers, we can see a hint of what I have meant to capture above. The title of this chapter is taken from William Shakespeare's most famous play, *Romeo and Juliet*.

Shakespeare, writing in the late 1500s, set his play in the north of Italy in the 1300s, perhaps itself a testament to the deep currents

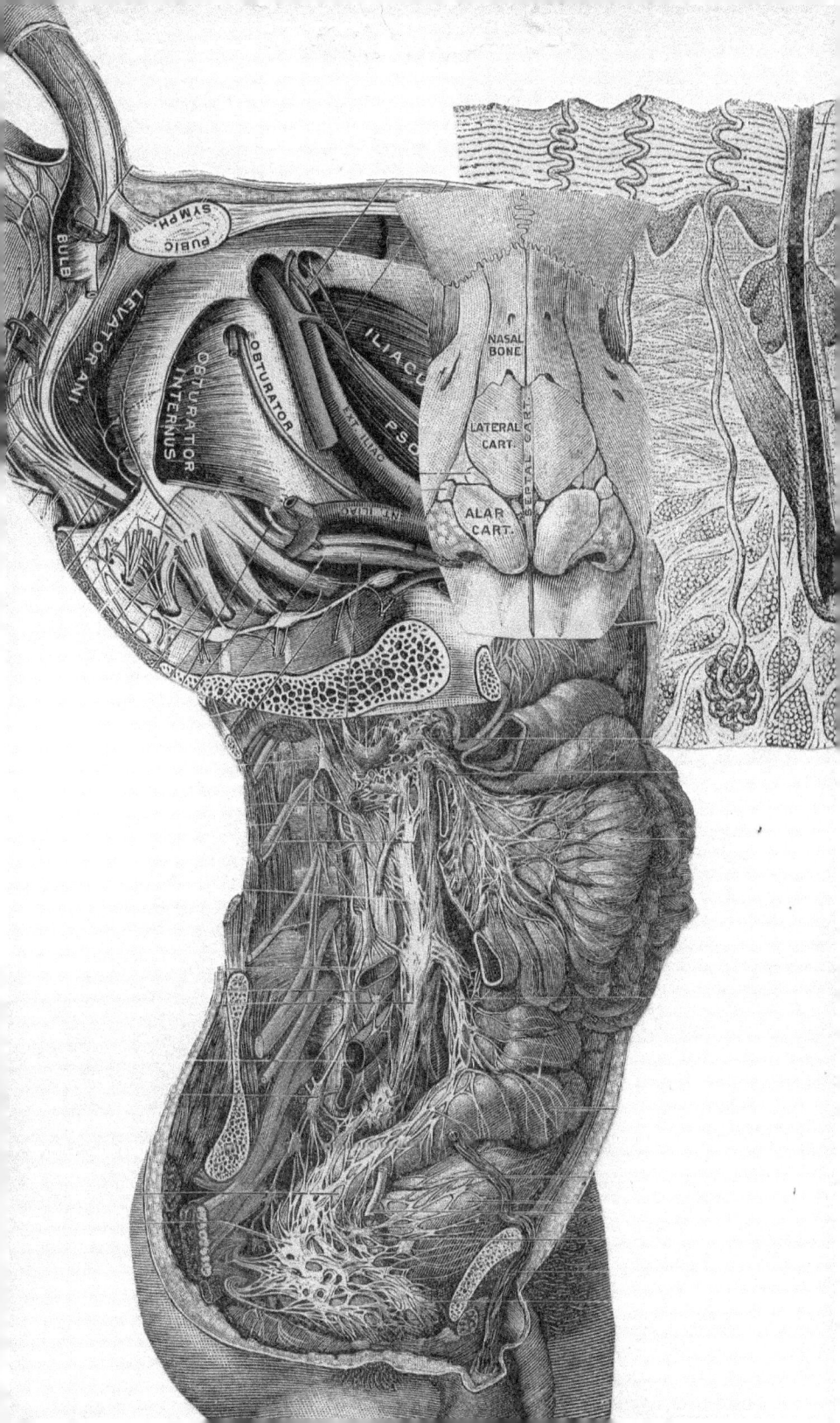

that guide human behavior but nevertheless seem beneath our ken. In his play, the young Juliet, doomed by her love, confounded by her desire for what she should not have, expresses a base and familiar frustration with the nature of the civilized world. In Act II, Scene II, poor, doomed Juliet asks with the pure honesty of youth:

*What's in a name?*
*That which we call a rose*
*By any other name would smell as sweet.*

Indeed. Surely the sweet scent of a rose is not determined by the English, Italian, or Latin name one might assign it. The smell of a rose transcends what we can call it and exists independently, beautiful and without need for our order.

Juliet, of course, is referring to her family and to the rival family name of Romeo. She explains to Romeo with dangerous candor that a family name has nothing to do with their love, and while family names have little to say in this chapter, love and beauty, via olfaction, do just as Juliet knew it then.

Why should a man smell of gunpowder and tobacco? Why would these ingredients specifically attest to masculinity or even act as a gentle aphrodisiac? Why, centuries before in an imagined Italian village, would a woman stung by bitter love think to compare her lover to the profound and universal beauty found in the subtle sweetness of a rose?

Odor, it turns out, has everything to do with the formation of social hierarchies, and to the selection of sexual partners.

## GLADIATORS

Walking in modern-day Rome, even in its quietest moments, brings a peculiar feeling of stepping through untold layers of chiseled history: the cobbled alleys, the frenetic energy, the buildings that rest upon buildings that rest upon buildings. I remember some years ago, while walking up a gentle slope away from the steep banks of the Tiber, I traced the soft curve at the base of the Palatine hill. It was August, and the heat was like pressure both bearing down from the oppressive sun and reflecting up from the dark stone pavers. It was stifling.

As I ambled slowly along the base of the hill, the day building its oppression, I found myself suddenly tracing the contours of the Circus Maximus. Perhaps it was the stifling heat, or perhaps the stress of travel made my mind a bit fuzzy, but I swear that I could feel the history of the place. It was as if I could hear the clamorous frenzy of the crowd still echoing from the stones. I pressed further around the hill and came out to the arch that leads directly toward the Colosseum, and the illusion took me over completely. It required no imagination at all, standing beneath the rhythmic arches, to feel that I could be among the multitudes walking this precise path on the way to some bloody event some nineteen centuries previous.

In its time, the Roman Empire was one of the greatest civilizations in human history. Its expansive reach held jealously and violently to regions from North Africa to Britain, Portugal to Asia. And here I was, standing against the same stones that once hosted the most notable and vicious symbols of that empire: gladiators. I pictured their feet standing where mine were now. I imagined the bustle and noise of the day. I felt like one of those masses, sweating through my clothes as I pressed up the slope in hope of finding some cool shade beneath the looming stone structure. To think of the people who had come here, to think of the countless people who had fought and died here. It was a staggering focal point and symbol of an extraordinary time and an extraordinary people.

Imagine the spectacle. Standing in the shadow of the Colosseum, I could feel what it must have been like, in equal measures dumbstruck by the architectural brilliance of the structure and in raucous reverence of the gladiator himself. It was a filthy and horrible business.

The gladiators captivated audiences during a span of hundreds of years. While early combatants were usually conquered peoples and slaves, eventually, free men and ex-soldiers were lured into the arena, intoxicated by the thought of prize money and the potent glory of the gladiatorial games. Despite their lowly origins, the successful combatants were often treated like celebrities. Some enjoyed noble sponsorships and other lucrative endorsements. Toy figures of their likeness and public portraits were found across the twisting streets and shaded, pungent alleyways.

Some of the most famous gladiators were sex symbols of their time, and their blood and sweat were collected and sold as coveted souvenirs. Wealthy women dipped their jewelry in gladiator blood, and gladiator sweat was mixed into women's facial creams and used as an aphrodisiac.

As I stood there, my shirt soaked through from the heat, I considered the peculiar irony that within the social hierarchy, gladiators could be both lowly and scorned but also revered by the very nobles, senators, and merchants who would gather to watch them slaughter one another.

This story, like the heat and sound from the stones, also echoes across time and reaches us today. It is quite often true that there is simultaneous adulation and scorn for modern-day fighters. It suggests that something deep and perhaps dark resides within our human consciousness that one might admire and even wish to have the steely courage to stand across the red sand of the Colosseum, feel the same sun, hear the nobility clamor their name, and find the courage to fight.

Of course, we like to believe ourselves more civilized, culturally distanced from the orgiastic bloodlust of ancient Rome, yet a simple browse through the catalog of Western cinema suggests that bloodlust is still in style. The thirst for violence can be found in the contemporary imagination of Rome itself, through films like *Gladiator*, *Ben Hur*, and *Spartacus*, to name just a sample from across Hollywood's fixation.

But why?

Whether we like it or not, whether we admit it or not, the fight-or-flight response is exceptionally strong in humans. We feel it in our spine, the bottom of the stomach, and we know it on some liminal level, perhaps just beyond our understanding. Just as I remember standing beneath the looming mass of the Colosseum on a sweltering August morning, something else within us still stands in the shadow of that violence and recognizes it.

## MAJOR HISTOCOMPATIBILITY COMPLEX (MHC)

Was it fanciful to imagine myself sweating in the oppressive heat of an ancient Roman festival in August? Perhaps just as fanciful as imagining that Juliet could possibly have selected Romeo because of her preference for an MHC-dissimilar mate.

What would we call MHC if by any other name?

MHC is the initialism for major histocompatibility complex, which is a tremendously complex way to describe a selection of genes that have a peculiar task involving the immune system's ability to distinguish and differentiate between self and nonself cells. *Histo* means tissue, so we can think of it as tissue compatibility. To put it more simply, MHC is a molecule on the outside of immune cells that presents information on the health of the cell, which the immune system uses to check for disease. MHC molecules exist within all of us and are diverse: no two individuals have exactly the same set of MHC molecules (except identical twins). This means that a population won't fall victim to a brand-new or modified virus because at least some people will be able to mount an immunological defense.

That is all quite a lot. So let's trace our steps down the hill and think this through with an example so simple that it is also staggeringly beautiful, the way simple truths are.

In 1995, at Bern University in Switzerland, an innovative researcher named Claus Wedekind did something that might not seem particularly scientifically compelling. He asked college-aged males to wear t-shirts overnight for several days without washing, using scented soaps of any kind, or wearing deodorant or cologne. Just men and shirts. Although these men were by no means gladiators, Wedekind wanted those shirts to absorb the unnamed scent of the young students as purely as possible.

Wedekind collected these shirts and asked females of the same age range to press the shirts to their faces and smell each. The women then categorized the odors of the shirts as either pleasant or unpleasant (these were all women who had consistent, normal menstrual cycles and were asked to rate the t-shirts during the follicular phase of their cycle, when a woman is most likely to become pregnant).

Wedekind found that females rated the odors of the MHC-dissimilar (the molecules that were more different than her molecules) men as more pleasant than the MHC-similar men. He hypothesized that women prefer the odors of MHC-dissimilar men because they are less likely to be related individuals (which would help avoid inbreeding) and because it would enhance the MHC diversity of their offspring (making healthier children). According to the "good genes as heterozygosity" theory, females should favor mating with more heterozygous men in order to produce more heterozygous (and fewer inbred) offspring.[28]

Perhaps Juliet used her sense of smell to determine that Romeo had an MHC odor that was dissimilar to hers. It makes the love story even more compelling. The gladiator sweat that women purchased may have also contained odors of MHC-dissimilar men, thereby attracting the women whose complex biologies sought to produce healthier children.

## MICE

Humans are not alone in the use of chemical communication. In fact, chemosensation (the ability to perceive and respond to chemicals in the environment through smell) and chemoreception (the ability to perceive and respond to chemicals in the environment through taste) are some of the most primitive senses. As it turns out, we see MHC-based sexual selection in a breadth of otherwise dissimilar animals, including humans, primates, other mammals, birds, fish, and reptiles. Male and female mice, for example, often choose MHC-dissimilar partners.

Sex pheromones also play a role in rodent mate selection. Sex pheromones are pheromones that an organism releases to entice another member of their species to mate with them or to carry out other tasks that are closely related to sexual reproduction. Female mice prefer to mate with dominant males. Females are able to smell male pheromones. When the female mice smell this odor it causes endocrine changes in their bodies that subsequently lead to changes in their mating behavior and reproduction, selecting for dominant males. As we will see later in the chapter, human females also select for certain types of mates based on chemical changes occurring in their bodies in response to their monthly cycle.

## PHEROMONES

Scent has played an enormous role in human success and survival. We rely on our olfactory sense not only to avoid danger and not only to discover foods and pheromones, but also to help shape our understanding of attraction, sexuality, gender, and the bittersweetness of love.

If you were to fire up Google right now and type *aphrodisiac* into the search box, you'd get a bunch of results primarily involving foods. If you were to then click on the shopping option, a dizzying list of products would glow before you, including drops, drinks, herbs, elixirs, juices, teas, supplements, tinctures, essential oils, perfumes...you get the idea. The word aphrodisiac comes from the Greek word aphrodisiakos, which means "inducing sexual desire" and comes from *aphrodisios*, which pertains to Aphrodite, the goddess of love and beauty.

The word pheromone also comes from the Greek *pherein* (to bring or carry) and *hormon* (to excite). Scientists Karl Grammer, Bernard Fink, and Nick Neave stated that "pheromones are referred to as 'ecto-hormones' as they are chemical messengers that are emitted into the environment from the body where they can then activate specific physiological or behavioral responses in other individuals of the same species."[29]

Pheromones are released from glands located in the face, armpits, nipples, anus, and genitals. Androstenone—a pheromone that is found in the urine and sweat of humans—is found in higher concentrations in males than in females; it also signals dominance and draws attention. Therefore, it is often referred to as the "alpha male" pheromone.

If androstenone is more frequently associated with males, androstenol can be considered the female pheromone. One study has indicated both men and women exposed to androstenol rated photographs of women as more sexually attractive.[30]

Yet another pheromone is androstadienone, which has been called the "love pheromone." It is found in greater concentrations in male sweat and can be detected by women. Androstadienone increases the heart rate and feelings of closeness, intimacy, and appeasement in women. A study by Paavo Huoviala and Markus Rantala found that androstadienone increases cooperative behavior in men.[31]

## BROWN LEMMINGS

Another species that uses pheromones to communicate is the brown lemming (*Lemmus trimucronatus*). Brown lemmings are small mammals (15 cm long) with reddish-brown fur, and males are about 5–10 percent larger than females. They inhabit the treeless environment of the arctic and subarctic alpine tundra in North America and Siberia. In the summer months, they tunnel among the grasses and sedges, and during the winter, they are found in mossy areas with permanent snow cover.

Brown lemmings are mainly solitary, with individuals of both sexes avoiding each other except for mating. During mating season males are known to box, squeal, flip themselves on their backs, and bite their opponents. Studies have revealed that females prefer the odor of the victorious male lemmings.[32] Females want to mate with dominant males and try to avoid males on the losing end of battles. Olfactory preference tests reveal that estrous (sexually receptive or "in heat") females, when exposed to the odor of the dominant and subordinate males, prefer the odor of the dominant male.

In brown lemmings, the role of female choice cannot be denied. Female brown lemmings follow alpha males and flee from subordinate males. Females also exhibit lordosis (a mating position in which the female tilts the pelvis and elevates the hips, ready to receive the male) more frequently with dominant males. The defeated males attempt more mounts of females, but dominant males have more successful mounts.

## MUSKOXEN

Olfaction plays a big role in the social behavior and reproduction of another, much larger mammal, the muskoxen. Muskoxen (*Ovibos moschatus*) are also arctic animals, native to the tundras of Alaska, Greenland, and Canada, and have since been introduced into Russia, Norway, and Sweden. Muskoxen are giant animals weighing as much as 400 kilograms (882 pounds). They have short legs and a long, shaggy, brown coat, both adaptations for living in such a harsh environment.

Muskoxen are sexually dimorphic, with males being larger than females. During the breeding season, males compete for dominance through a variety of behaviors, including headbutting, head swinging, roaring, and urinating on their own feet. The urine has a pungent odor, hence the name muskoxen. This is not the only form of chemical communication that muskoxen use. Males also have glands near their eyes that they use to mark objects by rubbing up against them.

The social hierarchy of the herd is decided by dominance, which is determined by fighting, posturing, and scent marking. Age is also a factor; animals that are too young or too old cannot become alphas. The sweet spot is six to eight years old. Lower-ranking males and old bulls leave the herd and form bachelor groups or become solitary.

Muskoxen alpha male bulls assert their place in the hierarchy in a number of ways. One way the dominant males do this is by rushing and sometimes colliding with subordinate males. Alpha males will also kick lower-ranking males with their forelegs, something they do to females during courting as well. Dominant males also feign copulation with subordinate males and sniff their genitals.

Lower-ranking males occasionally charge at a dominant male, hoping to defeat the alpha and improve their own status. Fighting males rub their preorbital glands against their legs, bellow, and display their horns prior to charging one another.

Once these dominance contests are determined, the victorious male attempts to control and defend the females in the harem from other males. Dominant bulls are more aggressive during the rutting season and make decisions for the group. But this all changes once the females become pregnant; at that point, they take charge and decide where the herd will travel and where they will rest.

Components of the glandular secretions of muskoxen have been broken down by Dr. Peter Flood, Professor Emeritus, from the Department of Veterinary Biomedical Sciences at the University of Saskatchewan. His analysis of the preorbital gland (which is found in both sexes but is much larger in males) secretion showed the presence of cholesterol, benzaldehyde, a series of straight-chain saturated gamma-lactones, and monounsaturated gamma lactone.[33] This scent has been described as "light, sweetish, ethereal," but it communicates something quite serious: it provides an olfactory cue to other males that threat behaviors and conflict are imminent.

The other scent emitted by muskoxen is the one that gives it its name, but it is not derived from a musk gland. The odor from the dominant males during rutting season derives from the preputial gland (located in the folds of skin around the genitals). When the males urinate, some of it is also sprayed on themselves and absorbed by the underwool on the abdomen. Dominant males smell the most pungent during the rutting season. The urine combined with the pheromones released from the preputial gland communicate something to the rest of the herd (although we do not know exactly what that is).

As we have seen in mice, brown lemmings, and muskoxen, chemical communication is incredibly important. These mammals all use chemical cues to find mates and form hierarchies. There is another mammal species that also uses pheromones to communicate things, that being *Homo sapiens*: humans.

## FEMALE CHOICE

Female choice is incredibly important when it comes to selecting a mate with whom to reproduce. Since women invest more physically through gestation, nursing, and parental care, they generally are more selective in choosing potential sexual partners. A study conducted in the Czech Republic revealed that women going through the fertile phase of their cycle prefer the odors of dominant males.[34] Dominant men have a tendency to gain higher socioeconomic status and resources, which could be invested in their mate and offspring. There is some evidence that suggests that males with high genetic quality may not invest as much time in parenting, hence the emergence of a mixed mating strategy in females.[35] Females seek high-genetic-quality males for short-term or extra-pair sexual partners but at the same time look for males who are willing to invest time and money into their offspring as long-term partners.

Males also respond to female chemical cues. It is said that human females have a concealed ovulation, but in light of recent research, that may not be entirely true. Females are only fertile for a brief period of time every month, so possible olfactory cues could be beneficial for potential mates. Scientists Saul Miller and Jon Maner examined whether fragrances that indicate a woman's state of reproductive viability directly affect men's biological processes involved in mating. Their study revealed that men who smelled the scent of women near ovulation had higher levels of testosterone than men who were exposed to the odor of a woman far from ovulation.[36] The results imply that men are sensitive to chemosensory cues to female ovulation and that this sensitivity is expressed in particular endocrinological processes that are known to encourage mating in humans and other species.

When a woman is ovulating, her sense of smell is heightened. With this increased olfactory sensitivity, females have also shown a preference for more symmetrical males. Studies conducted by Randy Thornhill and Steven Gangestad have shown that females rate the scents of males with greater bilateral symmetry as more attractive during the fertile window of their cycle.[37] Outside of peak fertility, females do not have a preference for more symmetrical males; it is only when a female reaches her maximum fertility that she has the preference for symmetrical men. Men, on the other hand, have no preference for more symmetrical females. Mammalian males, which include humans, following the parental investment theory pioneered by Robert Trivers, approach any copulatory interaction as a low-cost and high-benefit opportunity. "Parental investment theory specifically predicts that sexual selection stemming from variance in genetic quality will be strongest on males in species in which males invest less than females."[38]

Why should a female select for more symmetrical males only while ovulating? It is believed that bilateral symmetry is a marker for good genes. Individuals who are less symmetrical often have more medical conditions, suggesting a possible lower genetic fitness. Some of the most common bilateral features that are regularly measured in humans are eyes, ears, wrists, and thighs. Through sexual selection, symmetry does affect physical attractiveness, which in turn impacts mate attraction. Thornhill and Gangestad's research has also shown that more symmetrical men are larger in body size, are more muscular, have a greater number of sexual partners, are chosen more often as partners for extra-pair copulations, and more frequently bring women to orgasm.[39] Fluctuating asymmetry had no impact on the number of sexual partners that women had.

## COPULINS

Copulins are chemicals that are secreted in the vagina of some primate species, including humans and rhesus monkeys. The chemical composition of copulins is a mixture of primarily aliphatic acids, alcohol and hydroxy ketones, and aromatic compounds. A study conducted by Megan Williams and Amy Jacobson proposed that males may be primed by copulins to compete with one another and act aggressively in the presence of an ovulating female.[40] These copulins have been shown to increase a male's testosterone levels by 150 percent. Males rate the odors of the vaginal secretions (copulins) at ovulation as the most intense and pleasant.

## CONCLUSION

Our sense of smell is probably the most overlooked and undervalued of all the senses. While it is true that our olfactory receptors are not as robust as some of our fellow mammals', there is still much to unpack regarding human pheromonal communication. We are still incredibly ignorant about chemical communication in most living organisms, including humans.

Males and females must synchronize reproductive functions in order to optimize fecundity, which is a major factor in evolutionary success. All modes of communication should be used to maximize coordination. Pheromonal communication does contribute to that coordination, according to recent investigations. It seems to reason that an individual will be more evolutionarily fit if they produce more pheromones and are better at detecting them.

## PART II
# KINGS AND QUEENS

# FOUR
# ALPHA ICONS

*"I refer those actions which work out the good of the agent to courage, and those which work out the good of others to nobility. Therefore temperance, sobriety, and the presence of mind in danger, etc., are species of courage; but modesty, clemency, etc., are species of nobility."*

—BARUCH SPINOZA

## MONGOLIA

Why do you want to go there? No one goes east. All of the worthwhile places to visit and cool activities are in the West. You're crazy. You will never make it.

I almost didn't make it.

After completing some field work in Mongolia's Ikh Nart Nature Reserve, I decided to take a little side trip. I found someone in Ulaanbaatar to take me to Dadal, twenty-five kilometers south of the Russian border in Eastern Mongolia. In turn, Dadal is 515 kilometers away from Ulaanbaatar, roughly an eighteen-hour drive, though our journey took well beyond that. The driver was a very stubborn fellow who refused to use maps, so eventually we became lost as evening approached.

There were no hotels or places of shelter anywhere remotely close, so we had to sleep in the truck that night. I slept in the back of the truck, while the driver slept in the driver's seat. It was not a comfortable night's sleep, and at daybreak we were back on the road.

We made it to the river Onon Gol, which we crossed by a hand-drawn ferry. This was a beautiful area rich with birches and pines. We pushed ahead after our river crossing. We had to drive through some small creeks along the way, which clearly made the driver nervous. And sure enough, around midmorning, he took a line that I thought was suspect, and we got stuck crossing a tiny creek that was so small that you could jump across it.

Due to the language barrier, I could not communicate my ideas, thoughts, and frustrations. I was pleading with him prior to getting stuck to put the truck into four wheel drive. He refused, but in his defense, I don't know if he understood what I was trying to communicate with hand gestures and pointing at gear shifters. We tried pushing and digging to no avail. Over the course of three hours, we did not see another car. Finally, we located a traveler with a motorcycle, who returned later with a small tractor. With the tractor pulling and four of us pushing, we were finally able to get out—each of us covered in diesel soot.

On an overcast day, my mood was bright when we finally arrived in Dadal. I rented a small cabin next to the house of a retired schoolteacher for several nights. His son spoke English and was able to direct me around town. I asked the son if he could help me locate a horse to rent and a guide to take me to a location outside of Dadal. He agreed. The following morning, I got up early and went for a walk in the woods. We had breakfast at the homestay and then began our day. The son, Enkhbayar, helped me find two horses to ride and agreed to act as my guide for the day. We saddled our horses and were on our way.

They don't name horses in Mongolia: it is either a white one, a brown one, or a black one. Mongolian horses are small but tough, and mine was no exception. I picked a white horse that the owner had to catch with a lasso-type thing— a long wooden pole with a leather noose at the end—called a lasso-pole, or *uurga* in Mongolian. There is something refreshing about just getting on a horse and riding, where there are no fences, no boundaries, just a wondrous and expansive land. We rode for five hours straight, stopping at some beautiful sites surrounding the Dadal area: rivers, lakes, forests, and hills. We rode through the woods, over hills and creeks, on sand tracks, and through fields of grass. Though cold and overcast, it felt magnificent.

At one point, I cut my own path and rode alone to the top of a hill where there was a simple stone marker with an inscription chiseled into it: "Chinggis Khaan was born here in 1162." What an astonishing place to have entered the world. Behind the stone marker were tree branches and logs arranged vertically, leaning against one another in a circular configuration, similar to that of a teepee. There was blue cloth wrapped around some of the branches. This blue silk cloth, called hadag, is sacred in Mongolian culture. Hadags are always blue because that is the most sacred color, representing the eternal blue sky in Mongolia. They are used when greeting or saluting one another with honor and respect. I was fortunate enough to receive one upon completion of our fieldwork, which was quite an honor.

From this land, Chinggis Khaan went on to become a towering figure in human history. Most people in the Western world know Chinggis Khaan as Genghis Khan. In many ways he may be the most iconic alpha male who has ever walked on this planet.

## GENGHIS KHAN

Genghis Khan's birth name was Temujin. He was born with a blood clot in his hand, which, according to Mongol folklore, meant that he was to become a leader. He had a tumultuous childhood. During this time, Mongolia was ruled by many different tribal groups. His father was the leader of one of these clans or groups, the Borjigin clan. Temujin's father, Yesukai, was poisoned by a rival clan. Temujin returned home. After his father's death, the Borjigin clan broke up and the family was left to fend for themselves. This was a stressful time for the family: they were alone without a father/husband, living off of the land, hunting and foraging. The family life of Mongol herders was typically governed by a rigid hierarchy, and Temujin's half-brother Begter, being the eldest son, wanted to assume the role of the head of the family. Temujin resented him for this and for the fact that Begter was stealing and hoarding food away from the family. Temujin and his full brother, Khasar, hatched a plan and killed their half-brother via arrows, one shot from the front and the other shot from the back.

Around the age of twenty, Temujin was captured in a raid by a neighboring clan. He was temporarily enslaved but escaped and started to form fighting units. Temujin continued to build up his army; his leadership inspired loyalty that was unprecedented at the time. None of his generals deserted him, believing that one day he would unite all Mongols from all of the tribes under his rule. His first order of business was to avenge his father's death. He wiped out that tribe and many other tribes within central and eastern Mongolia. In 1190, Temujin suffered a defeat to one of his rivals, Jamuka, that would ultimately be a turning point, as the cruelty exhibited by Jamuka and his warriors turned public support and sympathy in Temujin's favor. By the year 1206, he had conquered most of Mongolia through brilliant military tactics and outstanding leadership. It was at this time that he took the name Genghis Khan, which means "universal ruler." This title carried with it not only political significance but also spiritual significance, as he was accepted as the supreme god of the Mongols.

Once Mongolia was firmly in his control, he began building an empire the likes of which had not been seen before. It is interesting to note that historians speculate that the motivation for expanding his empire may have been due to food scarcity and a growing population that needed to be fed. Within a few short years, Genghis Khan's armies took over territories in China and then moved west after the Shah Muhammad, leader of the Khwarizm Dynasty, beheaded a Mongol diplomat. Within several years, Khan destroyed the Khwarizm Dynasty and expanded his empire.

Genghis Khan was a visionary and an innovator. He installed a form of government and organization that transformed Mongolia from a nation of warring tribes to a unified empire. He outlawed kidnapping, which he recognized as a major cause of strife among different tribes. He created a system of laws and regulations that were derived from practical considerations rather than ideology and religion, as was the case in many other parts of the world. Genghis Khan understood the importance of religious tolerance, as everyone within his empire was free to practice any religion of their liking.

Genghis Khan emphasized the importance of self-control and avoidance of materialism. When it came to trade and communications, he built a network of postal stations across the empire that also served as places of lodging for merchants. He lowered and standardized taxes on goods. He altered hierarchies so that climbing the ranks within the military and government was based on meritocracy and not the usual nepotistic system based on the traditional lines of heredity or ethnicity.

Genghis Khan demanded that every ambassador be seen as a peaceful messenger, which was not a common practice in the world at that time, with ambassadors frequently being tortured and killed. Genghis Khan generally only attacked when provoked. People were given warning and the option to surrender and assimilate into the empire.

As science writer Don Lessem stated, "Rewarding loyalty, showing mercy, creating rigid order, abstaining from personal aggrandizement, and empowering his troops, Genghis built a world from scratch. He grew his empire with charisma, with charity, with cunning. His ability to adapt and incorporate innovations from other cultures was unmatched."[41] In the end, Genghis Khan's empire stretched from the Yellow Sea all the way to the Black Sea, encompassing nine million square miles of China, Central Asia, Persia, Russia, and Hungary. Genghis Khan died in 1227 when he was in his sixties. His burial site is unknown but it is believed to be somewhere close to the place of his birth near the Onon River. Legend has it that the funeral escort killed anything they encountered on the way to the burial site and that a river was diverted over the grave to avoid detection.

Genghis Khan had six wives and over 500 concubines. Geneticists focusing on Y chromosomes have been able to trace the lineage back to the male line of descendants of Genghis Khan, as the Y chromosome is passed down directly from father to son. It is likely that Genghis Khan fathered hundreds of children. Geneticists estimate that sixteen million males in Asia (0.5 percent of the Earth's male population) are genetically linked to Genghis Khan. Scientists Tatiana Zerjal and Chris Tyler-Smith stated that "increased reproductive fitness, transmitted socially from generation to generation, of males carrying the same Y chromosome would lead to the increase in frequency of their Y lineage, and this effect would be enhanced by the elimination of unrelated males. Within the last 1,000 years in this part of the world, these conditions are met by Genghis Khan and his male relatives. He established the largest land empire in history and often slaughtered the conquered populations, and he and his close male relatives had many children."[42]

What are some of the qualities that made Genghis Khan an alpha male? He was a wise visionary who was able to conquer threats by constantly innovating and adapting. He believed that the key to good leadership was utilizing self-control and moderation. He was a strict disciplinarian who created rigid hierarchies to expand his empire. He was a brilliant strategist who valued and rewarded loyalty and was able to show benevolence. He shunned luxury and did not like to sleep indoors. These are some of the reasons he became a heroic figure to his people, who ultimately loved and revered him. Genghis Khan was also a terrifying figure who, along with his armies, killed hundreds of thousands of people. I am not trying to dismiss or ignore this ruthless side; I am merely saying that he was much more than the barbaric brute he is often depicted to be.

Do alpha males exist in modern day human populations, or are human social systems too complex, fluid, and dynamic? The term itself is quite loaded, and many believe that it should only be used for nonhuman animal communities. If we were trying to identify someone as an alpha, what specific qualities or characteristics would they need to have? Could the term be used if an individual was an intelligent, respected, charismatic, confident, benevolent, courageous, coalition-building leader? What if this person was also physically strong and powerful and possessed great fighting abilities?

## MOULAY ISMAIL IBN SHARIF

We find another example of an iconic alpha male a few hundred years after Genghis Khan. Moulay Ismail Ibn Sharif was the Sultan of Morocco from 1672–1727, a fifty-five-year reign. He was also a charismatic leader who created a strong army. Moulay Ismail Ibn Sharif was known by two nicknames: in Europe he was known as the Bloody King for his treatment of Christian slaves and in Morocco he was known as the Warrior King. He was born in 1645 in Sijilmassa, close to the border of Algeria, the son of a prince and a Black slave.

Moulay Ismail Ibn Sharif rose to power under his half-brother, Moulay Rashid, who made him a governor. After the death of his brother in 1672, he declared himself the Sultan of Morocco. He faced many difficulties early in his reign, including many rebellions against him. Most notable of those who rose against him were his nephew, whom he defeated to take control of the city of Marrakesh, and his brother.

Moulay Ismail tried to stabilize his empire while constantly battling blizzards, rebel tribes, and the plague. In 1680, Moulay Ismail decided that he wanted to push out the English and Spanish (the Christians) from the country. He was successful in his campaign to force out the Christian presence from Morocco, but rebels continued their attempts to destabilize the empire. Finally, by 1693, Moulay Ismail Ibn Sharif defeated the Berber rebels, the last tribe not under his control.

Moulay Ismail created the first professional army of Morocco, the Black Guard, made up of Black slaves that he brought in from other countries. At its peak, the Black Guard numbered 150,000 men.

Moulay Ismail Ibn Sharif died in 1727.

Moulay Ismail Ibn Sharif possessed many of the same qualities that Genghis Khan had: they were skilled horsemen and possessed tremendous physical strength and extraordinary cleverness. They were also both known to be ruthless and cruel, and both killed many people. Both were adept at incorporating the best of other countries, cultures, and knowledge to improve aspects of their empires. They both created incredible armies.

Moulay Ismail Ibn Sharif had four wives and many concubines. He is estimated to have fathered between 868 and 1,171 children, the most of any one man in human history. Scientists Elisabeth Oberzaucher and Karl Grammer of the University of Vienna explored his prodigious totals by creating an algorithm to examine different models.[43] Through the use of computer simulations, they determined that Moulay Ismail could have achieved those numbers by having sex once a day for thirty-two consecutive years. They also discovered through the simulations that he only needed a harem of 65–110 women (based on many possible factors that could affect reproductive success, including breeding pool, cycle day, copulation, fertility, conception probability, fertilization, and offspring survival), not the 500 that had previously been estimated.

Moulay Ismail Ibn Sharif was able to unite a fragmented Morocco and foster an environment of stability and prosperity for his empire. He had a monomaniacal obsession with ruling and uniting his empire against his adversaries. He also built many ornate, complex structures throughout Morocco and supported the arts. Diplomatic relations, peace, security, and economic prosperity flourished under his rule. Moulay Ismail Ibn Sharif sat atop the social hierarchy of an empire because of his ability to lead, access to resources, army, ability to command fear and loyalty from his people, and access to abundant mating opportunities.

## CHARLEMAGNE

Charlemagne (or as he is also known, Charles the Great) is another example of an iconic alpha male. He was the emperor of the Carolingian Empire from 800–814. Charlemagne's father was a mayor who became the King of the Franks and groomed Charlemagne for leadership by engaging him in fields such as government and the military. When Charlemagne's father died, the Frankish kingdom was divided between Charlemagne and his brother Carloman, and sibling rivalry nearly ruined the kingdom until Carloman's untimely death in 771.

King Charlemagne had to unite his people, and he did so in part due to his success in war. Charlemagne was much more than just a warrior; as history professor Richard Sullivan stated, "the ideal warrior chief, Charlemagne was an imposing physical presence blessed with extraordinary energy, personal courage, and an iron will. He loved the active life—military campaigning, hunting, swimming—but he was no less at home at court, generous with his gifts, a boon companion at the banquet table, and adept at establishing friendships."[44]

Charlemagne was especially adept at establishing and maintaining relationships with powerful people within the kingdom and even outside of the realm. His success in diplomacy was just as impressive as his conquests during military excursions. Perhaps his biggest achievement was when he was crowned the Roman emperor in 800. But his reign was short: Charlemagne died in 814.

Charlemagne had five wives (although some historians suggest he had ten), many concubines, and at least eighteen children. He has been called the "Father of Europe" for good reason, but not for the reason you may be thinking. Charlemagne unified a splintered Western Europe and motivated a cultural and intellectual renaissance.

## CONCLUSION

We like to believe that modern society is civilized, educated, and evolved—that we no longer engage in the brutal aggression and sexual politics embodied in the alpha male. But what is an alpha male exactly? Was Genghis Khan? Eight million people alive today can claim to be his direct descendants. Did the human alpha die with him, relegated to the museums of our collective history? Or have we missed something vital, compelling, and astonishing about the alpha male? Is our society too fluid, too dynamic to reliably say who is and who is not an alpha male?

Human society is structured in a complicated and unpredictable way. An individual may be an alpha in certain settings, but in others he may rank quite low. Often being an alpha is a stressful position,

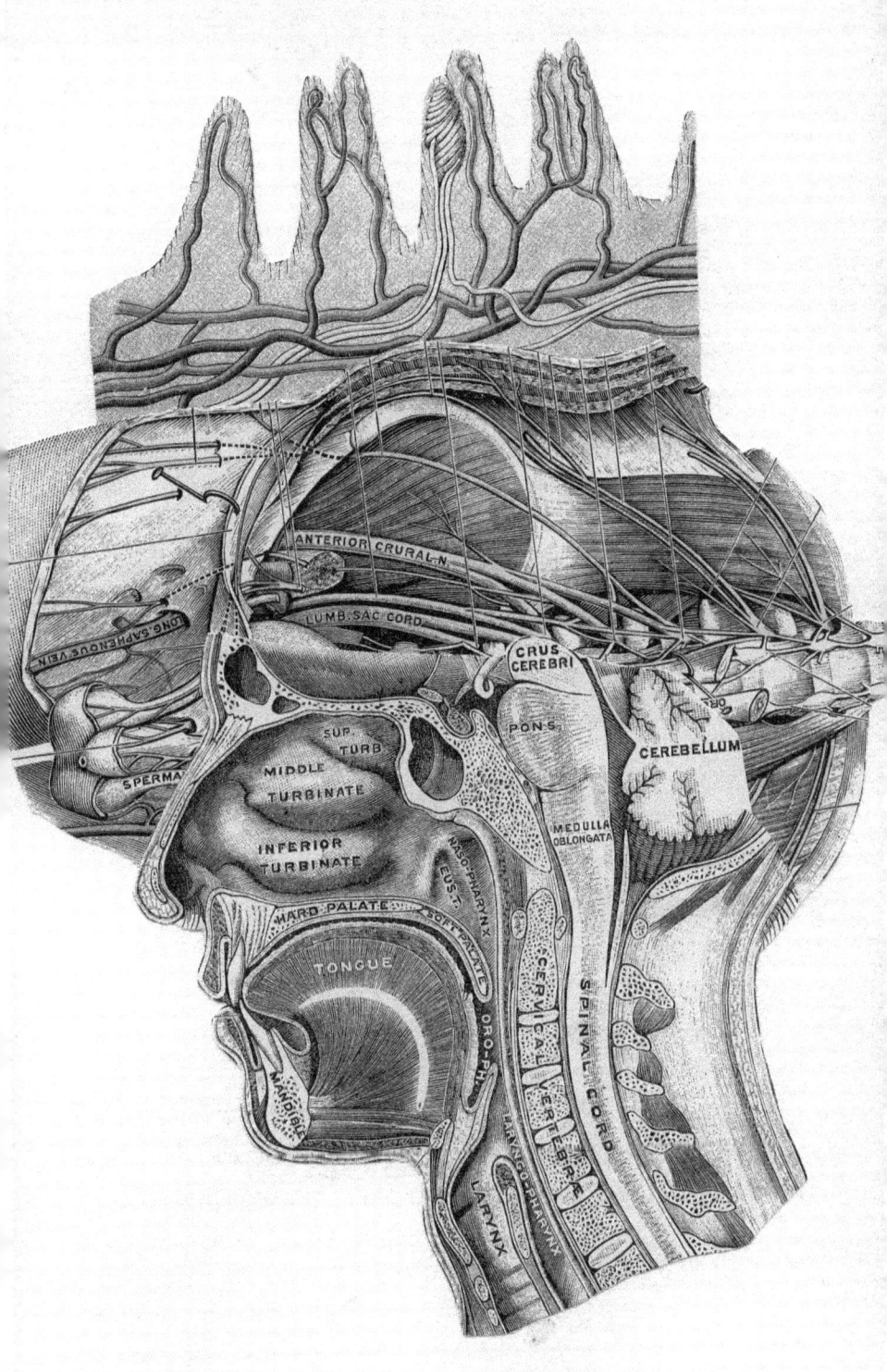

and the reign at the top is short. In fact, in many cases, beta males are just as successful as alphas, employing alternative reproductive tactics that cause far less stress. Beta may be the best strategy.

Could alpha males be in the process of being phased out? Sexual dimorphism in humans evolved because males had to fight each other for access to females. Males are bigger in most mammal species, but in monogamous species such as penguins and some other birds, males and females are exactly the same size. Humans fall somewhere in between.

It's worth pausing for a moment here and making an essential distinction. I've primarily been examining these three extraordinary individuals in positive terms, and this necessitates a quick caveat. I hesitate to distinguish the biological imperative from any consideration of the moral turpitude and extraordinary violence of each individual. Admittedly, I waver. Can we distinguish the biological from the ethical understanding of these individuals? We can see easily how this might spiral. Animals do not concern themselves with such moral matters—there is no such thing, for example, as murder in the animal world. There is only biological motivation. As humans, however, we distinguish ourselves precisely because we can conceive of violence or passivity in ethical terms. The animal kingdom remains instructive in that, at least.

My essential point here is simply that humanity is inescapably made of both worlds. We are human and animal. While I have observed here the remarkable nature of these individuals, I am focused on that biological level of instruction. The moral equation is another book.

Finally, as I recall that magical horseback ride in Dadal when I was transported back to the time when Genghis Khan himself rode over the same steppe, I remember feeling a great peace. I wonder if Genghis Khan—or Charlemagne, or Moulay Ismail Ibn Sharif—ever felt at peace. The immense stress and pressure that they faced on a daily basis must have been challenging; the price they paid, perhaps, for their places atop their respective hierarchies. As we will see in the next chapter, with both people and primates, the reign at the top of any social order is usually short-lived.

## FIVE
# PRIMATE POLITICS AND ALPHAS

"Now to what higher object, to what greater character, can any mortal aspire than to be possessed of all this knowledge, well digested and ready at command, to assist the feeble and friendless, to discountenance the haughty and lawless, to procure redress of wrongs, the advancement of right, to assert and maintain liberty and virtue, to discourage and abolish tyranny and vice?"

—JOHN ADAMS

## UNITED STATES POLITICIANS

In 1995, the United States Speaker of the House, Newt Gingrich, compiled his recommended reading list for incoming congresspeople. One of the books on his list was by a Dutch primatologist, Frans de Waal, titled *Chimpanzee Politics: Power and Sex Among Apes*. It was written in 1982 and was one of the first books to popularize the term *alpha male*. In it, de Waal describes the struggle for power among chimpanzees at the Arnhem Zoo. The book describes social hierarchies in chimpanzees and the formation of coalitions, betrayals, overthrows, and new leaders. As someone who did not always support science, it was a curious selection by Mr. Gingrich.

There is a lot of overlap with chimpanzee and human behaviors regarding the structure and formation of social hierarchies, and in many ways, both President Clinton and Speaker Gingrich acted very much like the chimpanzees de Waal described in his book. In fact, politics in this country is very much about hierarchies and the struggle for power.

The presidential race of 1988 pitted George Bush against Michael Dukakis. The voting populace and the media continually made fun of Dukakis's height (he was 5' 8" tall, while George Bush was 6' 2"). But the average height for the American male is only 5' 9". I think this shows how sensitive humans are to the perceptions of power.

Dukakis's height once again haunted him during a dubious staged photo op. His team thought that it would be a good idea to have him ride around in an eight-foot-tall M1A1 Abrams tank.

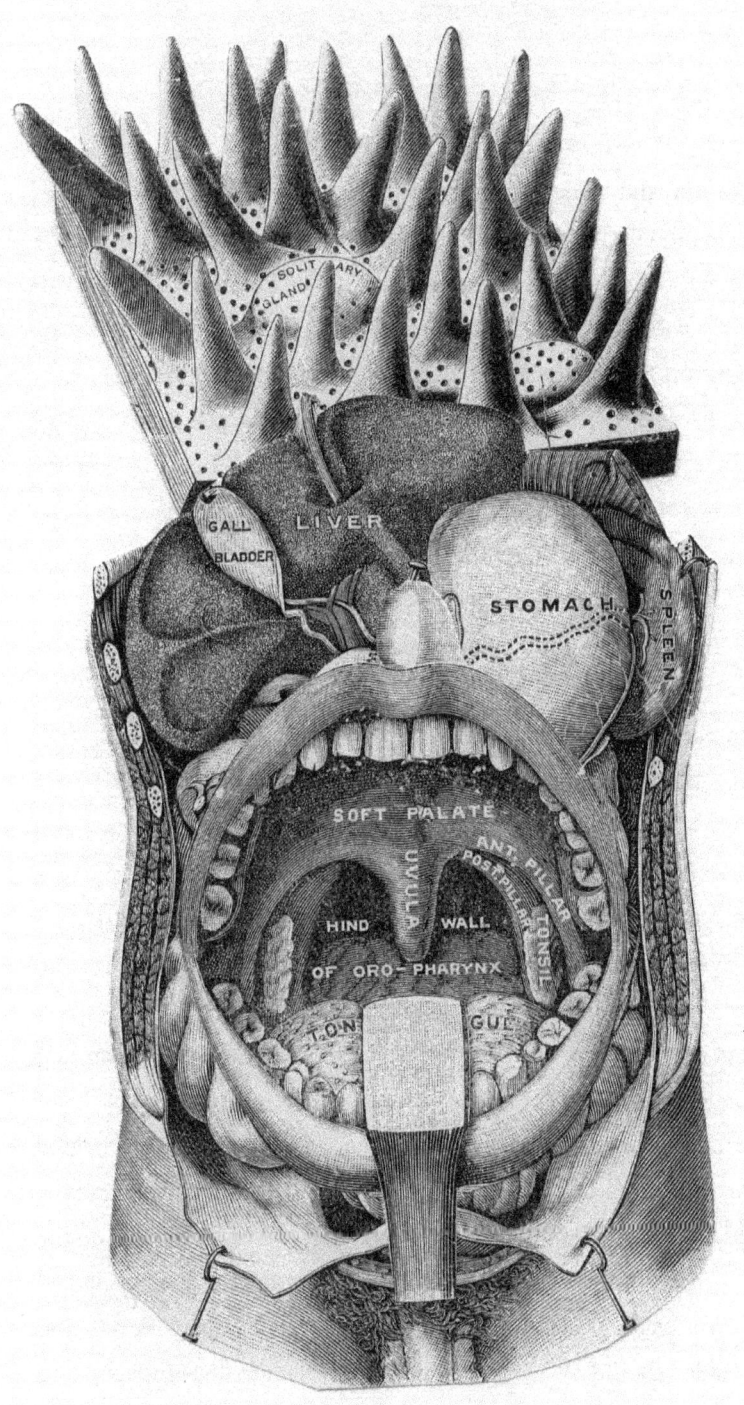

Not only did he get lambasted for the unflattering imagery of him trying to climb up the tank, but once he got inside and put on the helmet with his name taped on it, he looked diminutive and foolish.

One of the sound bites created by Bush's communications director, David Demarest, after the photo op was that "sitting in a tank does not make America stand tall." One poll found that 25 percent of respondents reported they were less likely to vote for him after the tank ride. He got caught pretending to be something that he wasn't.

## KAUTILYA

Human politicians hire political advisors to avoid the folly that ensnared Dukakis. One of the earliest political advisors was the Indian philosopher Kautilya (also known as Chanakya and Vishnugupta). He was a renaissance man, not only working in the field of philosophy but also as a minister, teacher, economist, advisor and a jurist. Kautilya wrote his seminal work *Arthashastra* in the third century BC to help young political leaders rule effectively. It is over 800 pages in length, with half of it devoted to war and foreign policy.

Kautilya was a skilled minister and advisor who helped Chandragupta ascend the throne and establish and then expand the Maurya Empire. His teachings and guidance were predicated on the assumption that war is a constant element among lands ruled by monarchs and kings. One of the major tenets of his work was that a leader should always aspire to expand his territory independent of any moral or religious constraints. As a matter of fact, Kautilya actively promoted preying upon religious or superstitious beliefs to further the goal of expanding territories. Kautilya espoused the use of concealed traps at places of worship, in which statues or stones would fall on unassuming worshippers. He also suggested using poison at frequent touch points or sprinkling it over gifts to assassinate enemies. Once again, at the core of his teachings was that nothing should quell the desire to expand one's territory because the size of the empire can inform the power it wields.

One of Kautilya's key contributions to statecraft was the theory of mandala. Mandala is a Sanskrit word that loosely translates to "circle." Mandala holds a great deal of symbolism in Hindu and Buddhist cultures. Many variations of mandalas exist; however, most are a series of circles within a square, arranged in groupings around a central point.

In the realm of politics, history professor William Frederick stated that "the mandala was not so much a territorial unit as a fluid field of power that emanated, in concentric circles, from a central court and depended for its continued authority largely on the court's ability to balance alliances and to influence the flow of trade and human resources."

The significance of the mandala is found in political formations, with the king's state being surrounded by circles of friendly and hostile states. We see evidence of the mandala in modern politics as a system of diffuse power based on interpersonal connections. The mandala is also still applicable to international politics with regards to foreign policy and diplomacy. Kautilya's mandala theory says to approach neighboring states as natural enemies and that weaker states should form coalitions with nations of equal status to protect themselves from superpowers that adopt expansionist strategies. We see these play out in modern nations throughout the world.

## MACHIAVELLI AND RHESUS MACAQUES

Kautilya's *Arthashastra* is often compared to Machiavelli's *The Prince*, but this characterization misses the mark. Machiavelli's work focuses on royalty and maintaining the monarch's power, whereas Kautilya stated that "the king is required to benefit and protect his citizens, including the peasants." Kautilya specifically mentioned the need to take care of and empower the weak and poor in one's kingdom. Machiavelli did not concern himself with the "lower classes" of society.

Machiavelli and Kautilya are similar in that both espouse the use of subtle, cunning, deceptive, unscrupulous, expedient, often murderous, and otherwise immoral pursuit of political power. They may very well have outlined the fundamental social attributes that have made *Homo sapiens* the most "successful" animals on an often unforgiving and complex planet. Humans are devious creatures, whether we want to be or not. More importantly, we may owe our global evolutionary success to this socio-political cunning.

Second in scope and breadth only to *Homo sapiens*, among primates, the ubiquitous rhesus macaques (*Macaca mulatta*) have genuinely conquered the world.

Rhesus macaques are found in India, Bangladesh, Myanmar, Thailand, China, Afghanistan, and Pakistan. After humans, rhesus macaques have the largest geographic range of all primates. Rhesus macaques also share many psychological and behavioral traits with humans, shaped by intense social interactions. The ambitious social structures of rhesus macaques might teach us a great deal about our own

Rhesus macaques use Machiavellian intelligence in their wondrously complex web of social stratifications. The monkeys make and break alliances, establish and absolve rules, flatter, lie, blame, and forgive just as humans do. Female rhesus macaques form powerful, rigid alliances within the social hierarchy. Some female macaques are born into a life of nobility and privilege, while others form shrewd networks of alliances to climb the social ladder.

In India, rhesus macaques are found throughout the country, from dense urban centers to more rural areas as well as in undeveloped habitats. In fact, rhesus macaques and humans often live in surprising proximity. Interestingly, the interactions between rhesus macaques and humans have an increasingly socially competitive edge, as was the case with a deputy mayor in New Delhi who died after falling from his terrace during an altercation with rhesus macaques.

The physical proximity between humans and macaques also exposes a fundamental correlation between social systems. Although India has legislated against "caste-based" discrimination, the practice of rigid social stratification continues to this day. In the caste system, we can see a clear example of human society organizing around an intensely potent hierarchical system. While perhaps an extreme example, such forceful social stratification was entirely familiar to Kautilya and Machiavelli, and it's hauntingly similar to any number of examples from modern "enlightened" democratic societies.

Power is the key. In the mid-1930s, a researcher introduced captured Asian rhesus macaques to Cayo Santiago, a small island off the coast of Puerto Rico, for the purposes of research and observation. The result was a bloodbath. Removed from any semblance of hierarchy and social order, the macaques went about an astonishingly violent process of redefining their social world. A short history of power, dominance, and violence occurred as the rhesus macaques were busy creating their own functioning order. Dominant individuals assumed their position, and the remaining rhesus macaques formed the basic outlines of a competitive pecking order. Various groups formed, and a secondary set of dominant hierarchies formed between groups. Amid the carnage, some order emerged, and over 200 new macaques were born. The rhesus macaques were eventually successful in establishing a new hierarchy and thus creating a functional society.

The large brain sizes of humans and rhesus macaques have allowed both species to live in complex societies with varied and interactive communication systems to be successful, dominant species. Other determinants of dominance include sex and age—where male macaques are usually dominant over females and adults are dominant over juveniles. Social group strength and structure also influence dominance.

Dr. Dario Maestripieri of the University of Chicago has studied primates around the world for over twenty years. Dr. Maestripieri has studied the rhesus macaques of Cayo Santiago for many years, and that was the impetus for his book *Macachiavellian Intelligence*, which explains the complex societies, hierarchies, and social bonds of rhesus macaques. Rhesus macaques display behaviors that are Machiavellian in nature and mirrored by behaviors in humans. We have all witnessed humans engaging in behaviors such as deception, manipulation, and exploitation of others for achieving social success. Humans and rhesus macaques use tactics not unlike those used by politicians today, or during the Renaissance or Kautilya's time.

Maestripieri contends that Machiavellian intelligence may be the reason both humans and rhesus macaques have been so extraordinarily capable in our respective conquest of the globe. Maestripieri argues that social and psychological factors, perhaps as much as evolutionary ones, deserve proper attention. Machiavellian intelligence (or as it is also known, social brain hypothesis) emphasizes social complexity as a driving force in brain evolution. Why have humans and rhesus macaques been so successful? The social brain hypothesis postulates that primates developed bigger brains to deal with the increased complexities of life. It works out like this: bigger social groups create complex social relationships, which in turn brings a suite of cognitive challenges. Handling all these cognitive challenges requires a larger brain. Humans evolved to have the largest brain of all primates to meet the social demands of large-group living.

Rhesus macaques also have large brains, but smaller than humans and other apes. They also form large social groups, but not as large as humans. Rhesus macaques have been incredibly successful but not as successful as humans, perhaps because their cognition, culture, and cooperation are not as robust.

Is it possible that non-Machiavellian traits and behaviors are also responsible for the success of humans and rhesus macaques? Maestripieri stated, "Our Machiavellian intelligence is not something we can be proud of, but it may be the secret of our success. If it contributed to the evolution of our large brains and complex cognitive skills, it also contributed to the evolution of our ability to engage in noble spiritual and intellectual activities, including our love and compassion for other people."

I think these dovetail with the social brain hypothesis, which argues that primates evolved to have larger brains to cope with an environment that is more complicated, both socially and otherwise. The cognitive abilities of rhesus macaques and humans have allowed them to propagate across the globe.

While researchers ponder the origins of global expansion, we can look to social hierarchies for other interesting impacts on behavior. Dr. Jenny Tung discovered that dominance rank impacts gene regulation, and in many primates, an individual's rank can have a tremendous effect on their health. As Dr. Tung stated, "In settings in which hierarchies are strongly enforced or subordinates have little social support, low dominance rank can lead to chronic stress, immune compromise, and reproductive dysregulation."[45] Low-ranking rhesus macaques often experience compromised heart health and endocrine function, as well as gene expression. We know that in humans, social stress and socioeconomic status also impact health. Dr. Tung was able to "provide genome-wide experimental evidence for the idea that social hierarchies polarize the immune system response toward a pro-inflammatory, antibacterial phenotype in low-status individuals and an antiviral phenotype in high-status individuals."

Social status can also increase mating success. However, mating success does not always translate into reproductive success. Dominant male rhesus macaques have a greater number of mating opportunities and also sire more offspring. Males also need to be smart enough to form alliances with other males and females so that they can count on their assistance during fights. These political alliances are necessary to build power and form coalitions.

Female rhesus macaques are also Machiavellian in that they mate with the alpha male out in the open at the most fertile stage in their cycle, but they also mate with other males discretely to reduce the chance of infanticide.

Both humans and rhesus macaques are both intrinsically selfish in that individuals use other individuals to their own benefit when necessary. Both are highly nepotistic and despotic societies, especially when it comes to politics. But humans have a better chance of rooting out these tendencies given that we have larger brains and are more innovative and are more cooperative as a species.

## SAVANNA BABOONS

In general, ranking high within a hierarchy is beneficial for a number of reasons, including greater reproductive success and higher growth rates (in other words, they reach maturity quicker, and more of their offspring survive). Social hierarchies also impact health, both negatively and positively. Stress induced from one's rank within a social hierarchy can activate endocrine reactions, including the release of glucocorticoids by the adrenal glands. Now, in the short term, this is a good thing because it creates the energy needed to take on the stressor, however, long-term exposure can suppress the immune system.

Scientist Laurence Gesquiere found that in savanna baboons (*Papio anubis*), alpha males have high testosterone levels and high glucocorticoid levels, while other high-ranking (but not alpha) males have high testosterone but low glucocorticoid levels. This suggests that there is a price to be paid for being king of the mountain.[46]

Both alpha and beta males receive about the same amount of grooming from females. Alpha male baboons differ from beta male baboons in that the alphas burn up much more energy guarding fertile females and fighting with other males. But scientists have found that alpha males are not great at monopolizing access to reproductive females; beta males have almost as much reproductive success and far less stress. Male savanna baboons at the lower end of the hierarchy pay the price in a different way; they expend a lot of energy trying to gain access to resources such as food.

Among savanna baboons, alpha males not only obtain more mating opportunities, but they also produce more offspring. Dominance rank is only part of the success of alpha male baboons. They also must be good at discriminating between fertile and non-fertile females.

Another interesting study conducted by Dr. Tung has shown that high-ranking male savanna baboons age quicker than other individuals.[47] Male baboons attain their highest rank between seven and twelve years of age. Individuals that do achieve a high rank within the social order generally experience a precipitous drop in status past the age of twelve. As Jenny Tung states, "In humans and other mammals this variation in aging shows up in chemical modifications known as DNA methylation marks." Clearly there are costs to being the top dog in the social hierarchy: in baboon males, their reign at the top is short-lived and also exacts a toll via epigenetic aging.

## CHIMPANZEES

We will end this chapter as we began: with renowned primatologist Frans de Waal and chimpanzees. Within every chimpanzee group there is one alpha male who is the highest-ranking male, and there is one alpha female who is the highest-ranking female. Although de Waal popularized the term *alpha male* with his book *Chimpanzee Politics*, it has been mischaracterized over the years. Some people think of alpha males as bullies, but this is simply not the case.

Dr. de Waal gave a TED talk in which he described alpha males in chimpanzees and related the concept back to humans. Chimpanzees often use body language to communicate status within the hierarchy, with alpha male chimpanzees often using a bipedal swagger (and we have all seen human males doing a similar type of strut). Alpha male chimpanzees "need to be impressive and intimidating and demonstrate your vigor on occasion and show that you are very strong, and there's all sorts of ways of doing that."[48]

Alpha male chimpanzees need to be generous and good at forming coalitions with others, especially females and older males. According to de Waal, unity is important, and coalitions stand together and walk in unison: "Demonstrating unity is extremely important in a coalition system." De Waal relates this to American politics during the primaries when the losers of one party must come together to support the victorious candidate. When a lower-ranking male chimpanzee attempts to overthrow an alpha male, he must campaign, similar to the way politicians do. He is very generous with food and affection, and he focuses on trying to win the support of the females within the group.

The biggest benefit of being an alpha male chimpanzee is having access to females. Ranking at the top of the social hierarchy improves their opportunities for sex and therefore their reproductive success. Food ranks below sex for alpha males. The alpha needs to keep his coalition members happy, especially older males, so he lets them mate with the females as well. To maintain his position, the alpha must be incredibly vigilant. Fending off rival males is very stressful and can take a toll both psychologically and physiologically.

De Waal emphasizes the obligations of the male chimpanzee alpha. The first obligation of the alpha male is to keep the peace among all members of the group in an impartial manner. His impartiality is what makes the alpha male popular within a group. The second obligation of the alpha male is to show empathy for other members of the group. Alpha males console distressed individuals and provide comfort during difficult times. We expect this from our human leaders as well.

Chimpanzees generally support good leaders and reject bullies. As de Waal stated, "You should not call a bully an alpha male. Someone who is big and strong and intimidates and insults everyone is not necessarily an alpha male. An alpha male has all sorts of qualities, and I have seen bully alpha males in chimpanzees, they do occur, but most of the ones that we have have leadership capacities and are integrated in their community, and like Amos at the end, they are loved and respected, and so it's a very different situation than you may think."

As we have seen with all the aforementioned primates, including humans, they all create social hierarchies that can be both beneficial and detrimental. We will never be able to fully divorce ourselves from social hierarchies, so the question becomes: how do we navigate hierarchies as social primates?

## XUNZI

Xunzi (also known as Xun Kuanag or Xun Qing) was a great Chinese philosopher who lived during the Warring States period (310–220 BC). Xunzi was one of earliest proponents of Confucian philosophy. One of his central tenets was that human nature is morally bankrupt and, when left to its own devices, will fall into violence and disorder. Xunzi is known for saying "human nature is bad." He believed that it was only through ritual that a society would remain stable.

Xunzi's philosophy was "the Way" or *dao*, which is a way of acting—the right way to live. He believed that when humans diverged from the Way, problems arose. Xunzi was unique in that he did not believe in heaven. He looked at heaven and nature in much the same way: that they neither help the good nor harm the bad. But rituals were of critical importance to Xunzi because he believed they bound society together.

Xunzi believed that if humans were good by nature, then there would be no need for rituals and social norms. He believed that people were essentially born with no natural concept of morality. Xunzi did not believe that humans enjoyed conflict; it was just a byproduct of their desires spinning them out of control. According to him, studying the Way and using rituals regulated human morality and desires.

Much of Xunzi's political thoughts were shaped by the period of time in which he lived. During the Warring States period, many states were warring with one another, trying to expand territories and power in hopes of creating a new dynasty. Xunzi, along with other philosophers of the time, believed that the government should be a monarchy. Poor kings should have a bad end, whereas a good, sage king following the Way could unify a country without winning a single battle.

Xunzi viewed social hierarchies as the key to maintaining order. When places within the social hierarchy become muddled and people step out of their roles, a breakdown occurs, with individuals indiscriminately trying to satisfy their desires. He contended that when people know their place within the social hierarchy and accept their role and benefits, they do not strive for goods beyond their standing. This will result in order and stability and will quell the competitive nature of humans. Once again, Xunzi emphasized the importance of ritual to social hierarchies, especially the obligations that people of different strata had to one another. The principles behind rituals help to sustain social hierarchies.

Xunzi believed that all humans fall prey to the impulse of desires. What is important is whether an individual acts upon those desires or exercises restraint. Ritual is the key because it teaches people to channel, refrain from, or even transform their desires to maintain social hierarchies.

As professors Daniel Bell and Wang Pei stated in their book *Just Hierarchy*, "The real moral value of hierarchical rituals, for Xunzi, is that they generate a sense of community among people with different power and status, and benefit both the powerful and the weak. Put differently, they can help to generate a sense of strong reciprocity among members of a hierarchical relationship, with the powerful and the weak coming to think of their fate as a common one. The bonds that hold them together are stronger than the fluctuating interests that underpin 'weak reciprocity.'"[49]

Xunzi's philosophies can also be applied to the social hierarchies that we see in primate communities, which benefit both strong and weak members. In some primate communities, higher-ranking members provide protection for lower-ranking members. Food sharing may also occur across a community's hierarchy. Cooperation among individuals of various ranks also occurs in primate social systems. Grooming also benefits lower-ranking members of the community. These types of interactions are all offshoots of the social brain hypothesis.

## CONCLUSION

We have learned from our primate brethren that they also play politics and have social hierarchies. Much the same as humans, these hierarchies are complex, changing, and dynamic social structures. From savanna baboons, we learned that being a beta may be the best spot within the hierarchy. This may be true for other species as well.

Both humans and rhesus macaques are Machiavellian in their social pursuits, as Frans de Waal showed us with chimpanzees. This challenges our notion of what it is to be an alpha male. What is an alpha male among humans? Does it even exist? The research on primate social structures can inform us on our social behaviors and patterns. The philosophies and tactics used by Kautilya in India, Machiavelli in Italy, or Xunzi in China many years ago are just as relevant today as they were back then. We need to be reminded of the folly of humans within our social hierarchies and learn from our own history as well as from other primates.

## SIX
# IT'S GOOD TO BE THE QUEEN

*"Women have served all these centuries as looking-glasses possessing the magic and delicious power of reflecting the figure of man at twice its natural size."*
—VIRGINIA WOOLF

### PENIS POWER?

"Suck my dick," shouted a female voice, and I turned my head. The moment caught me flat-footed. A woman was standing at a busy urban intersection, shouting across the street to another woman on the corner. I was cutting across one of the side streets that connected a former warehouse district to the main road. It wasn't the first time I'd heard a woman say that, and I'm certain it won't be the last, but the phrase still feels quite jarring to me. How interesting that women use that phase to insult others when they lack the very equipment required. A female friend has suggested that women say that it is empowering. Would it be more empowering to say, "Lick my pussy?" I struggle to think that this flows in both directions. Will we likely hear a man say, "Lick my pussy?" I can't quite imagine what that would mean. Some women that I have asked about the usage of "suck my dick" find the phrase crass and refuse to use it; other women have said that it is empowering and mocks patriarchy, and yet others just find it funny.

There's something really quite scandalous about it all—salacious, fun, insulting, and crass, for sure. When a man says, "Suck my dick" to another man, this is an insult. When a man says, "Suck my dick," to a woman, he is hoping that she will oblige with fellatio. When a woman says, "Suck my dick," to another woman, is it for humorous purposes, or is it also meant as an insult? When a woman says, "Suck my dick" to a man, is it meant to show that she is dominant over the man, or is it an insult (or both)? Do men and women believe that the penis represents power and the vagina represents weakness? Have we culturally internalized these structures in ways that we fail to see?

In the movie *Beasts of the Southern Wild*, there is an exchange between a father and his daughter in which he encourages her to say, "I am the Man." He does so to empower her. She is the Man. She dominates. She writes the rules for those around her. She is the alpha.

In life, who is "the Man?" Why does the Man need to exist at all, and where do women fit in a world where the Man writes the script?

This chapter will explore female dominance hierarchies, violence, and feminine energy in a variety of species, including *Homo sapiens*. To do so, let's rewind a moment to think about how this plays out in human history and in our social moment.

## **BLACK ANNA**

In 1524, throughout central Europe, the peasantry occupied the lowest rung on the societal ladder. The life of a peasant at this time was quite bleak: a peasant could not hunt, fish, or collect firewood on common land, as it was controlled by a lord. When peasants died, the lord took their livestock and possessions, including basic clothes and tools. If peasants wanted to marry, they needed approval from the lord and were required to pay a tax. These heavy taxes and duties placed on the peasants (who enjoyed few legal rights and no social mobility) largely inspired a rebellion that started in the German-speaking parts of the Holy Roman Empire.

Agrarian peasants from the southern and central parts of Europe joined the urban poor to fight against the status quo. It was a brutal rebellion, hard fought, with an understanding that there was little left to lose. Perhaps oddly, the rebels were not fighting to overthrow the government. Instead, the peasants offered a list of demands, some related to the church and others related to land access and justice system reform.

The princes of the Holy Roman Empire crushed the rebellion unceremoniously; of the 300,000 people who took part in the uprising, 100,000 were killed. It was a brutally fought contest with extraordinary cruelty on both sides, and once the rebellion was defeated, the rulers instituted laws that were even more repressive than the previous. It is referred to the Peasants' War of 1525, and although the rebellion was crushed, it remains a powerful symbol even 500 years later.

In 1903, a German woman named Kathe Kollwitz created a searing image of a heroine named Black Anna leading the uprising. Kollwitz's inspiration for creating this artwork came from reading Wilhelm Zimmermann's book *The History of the Great Peasant War*, in which he describes a peasant woman, Black Anna, who incited the revolt. I see Black Anna as a woman that had no need for hats and mugs emblazoned with the phrase "Suck My Dick" and t-shirts with the phrase "Stop Busting My Balls" and no need to trumpet the phrase "I'm the Man;" she lead with conviction and courage and happened to be a female doing so.

Black Anna was a catalyst for a rebellion in her time and demonstrated extraordinary potency in undertaking the Peasants' War. She remains a powerful symbol today in part because she seemingly undermines the concept of traditional sex roles. Kathe Kollwitz identified with Black Anna and created a series of etchings called *The Peasants' War (Bauernkrieg)*. One of the etchings, *Losbruch (Outbreak* in English), depicts Black Anna leading men into battle in a town called Heilbronn. Professor Linda Nochlin describes Kollwitz's *Losbruch* etching as "an image of excessive violence and feminine energy."

How did this woman, Black Anna, become a symbol of a conflict that was so exceptionally brutal? On the one hand, Black Anna shows us a perhaps non-stereotypical facet of the feminine persona, a persona not readily associated with merciless violence. Her power came in part from the unexpected nature of her brutality, and perhaps this quality makes her an extraordinary symbol today, as we relearn lessons that we might always have known: females of the species are no less potent, no less brutal, and no less dynamic for being female. To ignore this point is to miss so much about what hierarchy means, how selection works, and why this complex puzzle is so wondrously strange.

## PIPEFISH

Just as Black Anna assumed a sex-role-reversed position, female pipefish also take on more stereotypical male roles and are an example of a sex-role-reversed organism. Pipefish belong to the family *Syngnathinae*, which also includes seahorses and seadragons. They are similar to seahorses but have a straight body and long tail; they look like a slender pipe, hence the name pipefish. There are over 200 species of pipefish, and they can range from one to twenty-six inches in length. In place of the usual fish scales, pipefish have bony plates for protection. Some pipefish species have the ability to change color, allowing them to blend into their environment and avoid predation. Like their relatives seahorses and seadragons, pipefish have a fused jaw with a pipette-like snout that is used for sucking in their food. They feed on crustaceans, fish, and parasites, cleaning them off other fish. Most pipefish are weak swimmers in open water, hence they are generally found in shallow coastal waters seeking shelter among the reefs and grasses.

The broad-nosed pipefish or deep-nosed pipefish (*Syngnathus typhle*) is found in the Eastern Atlantic from Norway all the way down to Morocco. It is greenish in color with a yellow underbelly and averages six to eight inches long. Like other species of pipefish, the broad-nosed pipefish is sex-role-reversed. Females compete for access to males and males are choosy. Male broad-nosed pipefish possess a brood pouch (a slit that opens into a cavity where the female deposits her eggs to develop) on the underside of their bodies. Once the female deposits her eggs, the male releases his sperm into the pouch and then positions himself into a shape similar to the letter S to fertilize the eggs. The male then provides nourishment and osmoregulation for the fertilized eggs for about four weeks until the more developed hatchlings are released into the open water.

Female pipefish compete more intensely over mates than do males, exhibit sexual ornaments (a striped pattern), and usually initiate sexual behavior. Anders Berglund, a Norwegian scientist who has studied pipefish for many years, found that the male pipefish prefer females with ornaments.[50] The females that displayed the ornament for a longer period of time had greater mating success. It is costly for the females to display the ornament because it increases predation threat, and they may have less energy to invest in reproductive potential (meaning fewer or smaller eggs); therefore, it may be that only the largest alpha females can endure the energetic costs.

The courtship of deep-snouted pipefish goes something like this: Males search around the eelgrass looking for groups of females displaying. Males prefer to mate with the largest female they can find. Females prefer larger partners as well and compete with other females vigorously for desirable mates. Females who are competitive may be better able to repel attempts by other females to interfere with copulation. Once the female displays, the male may or may not dance. If the ritualized dance is performed and the other is receptive, then the two will come together and dance until the female delivers her eggs into the male's brood pouch.

Mate choice is important for any reproducing species, but it is especially interesting in deep-snouted pipefish because males are pickier than females. This is interesting because in most mammals, birds, lizards and fish, females are usually the ones doing the choosing. Large females seek out large males because they can transfer more eggs and they will have a greater chance of survival, while large males seek out large females because they produce a greater quantity of eggs that are also larger in size. Males also avoid females that have parasites that may compromise their fitness and reproductive potential.

Sometimes pipefish are unable to mate with their preferred partner, so both males and females have come up with strategies to compensate for their lackluster mate. Females transfer more protein-rich eggs when mating with a lower-quality male because the additional protein increases survival to the embryo stage. If a male copulates with a lower-quality female, he will absorb the embryos and will in turn have more resources for a large female.

The worm pipefish (*Nerophis lumbriciformis*) also displays interesting courtship behavior. The initial courtship is spurred on by an increase in activity by the female. She approaches the male, moving parallel to him, and begins to quiver. The female continues to quiver and moves slightly forward to see if the male follows. If he does, the female initiates contact with the male and continues to quiver. The intensity of the quivering reaches a point where the male's body may shake. During this initial courtship, many rival females try to disrupt the courting, but if the pair makes it through the disruption attempts, they then enter the spawning phase. The female once again initiates, moving her body so that her ventral side is facing the male. He responds by positioning his ventral side toward hers so that their genital regions are facing one another. As the genital regions come into contact, the male vigorously vibrates his dorsal fin, and the female deposits her eggs in the brood pouch. The final stage of the courtship is the embrace, which occurs immediately after spawning. The male initiates the embrace by wrapping himself around the female. They will remain embraced for ten to fifteen minutes. Scientist Nuno Monteiro and colleagues documented this courtship behavior in which females are the courting sex and, during reproduction, exhibit more pronounced changes in color patterns than males.[51] Additionally, they noticed that intruding females frequently interrupt mating, which is likely a sign of female–female competition.

Ultimately, the sex that limits the other's reproductive rate determines the role, and often the female limits the male; as a result, males compete for female partners. But as we have seen in pipefish, the roles are reversed, with females limiting the reproductive rates of males. The sex that has the higher parental investment generally equals the limiting resource. Male-only care is relatively common in fish because females "reward" males by spawning with them since they are already caring for a brood. External fertilization also lends itself toward male care since males can have a greater confidence of paternity. In addition, the type of parental care that is provided, such as fanning and guarding a nest with eggs, is not very costly to the male providing the care.

Another unique and interesting sex-role-reversed species is the spotted hyena. Like pipefish, female spotted hyenas are larger than their male counterparts and more dominant.

## SPOTTED HYENA

The African sun was rapidly descending in the sky as the driver, the park ranger, and I rumbled along off-road, making our way toward a cave that was known to be a home for spotted hyenas. I was quite excited because I had never seen a hyena in the wild. Hyenas are very interesting mammals, especially the females. If a female hyena were to somehow verbalize "Suck my dick," she'd certainly lay claim to such a phrase, as we shall soon see.

We parked the truck and began to walk in the general direction of the cave. We had to jump over fissures in the ground, which made for a hair-raising experience. One false jump or slip, and you'd fall down a chasm that reached untold depths. We found a rocky outcropping overlooking the massive cave, where we sat in silence as dusk descended upon us and the first hyena emerged from the cave. At first there were just some smaller juveniles, and then finally the adults came out. It was impressive and a bit haunting as they made their distinctive "laughing" sounds and scurried about.

After some time observing the hyenas, we started making our way back to the truck. As we crossed back over the fissures, bats flew out of them, creating a surreal experience. I thought about our early hominid ancestors and what they must have experienced listening to the cackling of the hyenas and watching the bats fly about in the night sky. I thought about their fears, their curiosities, their very survival in this land where modern humans have discovered evidence of their existence. The beauty and the mystery of the natural world is such a gift. We have so much yet to learn, experience, and understand.

The spotted hyena (*Crocuta crocuta*) is another species where females are dominant over males. Aristotle authored a book in 350 BC entitled *The History of Animals* in which he looked at many animals, including the hyena. He chose the hyena because at the time it was thought that they were hermaphrodites, but Aristotle performed a detailed dissection of the hyena, specifically the reproductive organs, and determined that they were not actually hermaphrodites.

Spotted hyenas are found throughout sub-Saharan Africa, except for equatorial rainforests and South Africa. They inhabit savannas, dry steppes, semi-deserts, and even mountainous forests up to 4,000 meters. Their fur ranges from sandy brown to slate, and their body is covered in irregular spots that fade as they age. Spotted hyenas are powerfully built, with massive necks and large heads and front legs longer than their back legs. They have robust teeth and possibly the strongest jaws of any mammal on the planet. Spotted hyenas dig their own burrows but also utilize communal caves.

Spotted hyenas are sexually dimorphic, with females (55–70 kg) outweighing males (45–60 kg). Females possess genitalia that look almost exactly like that of males—even well-trained field biologists have a hard time distinguishing males from females. The female "pseudo-penis" is actually an enlarged clitoris, and females even have a sac filled with fibrous tissue to mimic the testes and scrotum (made through the fusion of the labia majora). Females lack an external vagina, so everything occurs through the clitoris: mating, urination, and even birthing. As one can imagine, the morphology for this is not great, so the clitoris actually ruptures during the birthing process and then takes several weeks to heal.

The clitoris is even capable of erection. Both male and female spotted hyenas display erections during meeting ceremonies (which are not sexual). One individual approaches another, and the subordinate hyena lifts its hindleg for the dominant hyena to perform an inspection, both visual and olfactory, of the erect penis or clitoris. Females generally do not greet males in this way; they generally only perform the inspection for the highest-ranking males. Cubs are capable of performing meeting rituals at one month of age. Scientists hypothesize that the meeting ceremonies are correlated with the complexity found in spotted hyena social relationships, and they have also determined that high-ranking hyenas receive more meeting ceremonies than their lower-ranking counterparts.

University of California-Berkeley professor Stephen Glickman has done a considerable amount of research on spotted hyenas. He found that in spotted hyenas, coalition-building and dominance are partially fueled by aggressiveness, and this both allows and encourages high-ranking animals to engage in affiliative behavior and create strong social relationships.[52] This reinforces the matriarchal dominance hierarchy and continues within the social group and the species as a whole.

In spotted hyenas, female dominance is pervasive in almost all social interactions where questions of hierarchical order occur. Male spotted hyenas always yield to females. Females lead the packs, organize scent-marking expeditions, lead border patrols, and go to war. Both male and female hyenas mark their territories with deposits from anal scent glands.

Spotted hyenas live in clans that range in size from ten to ninety individuals. Spotted hyena societies rival the social complexity of many old-world primates. The clans are structured by rigid, linear dominance hierarchies, and an individual hyena's position within the hierarchy determines access to resources, especially food.

Hyena clans have a matrilineal organization, where social rank is determined by the mother's position within the hierarchy. Juvenile males leave the clan after puberty to join new clans. When a male enters a new clan, he is the lowest-ranking hyena in the dominance hierarchy and behaves submissively to all other hyenas in the clan. He only moves up in the hierarchy when an older male dies. Females maintain stable ranks within the hierarchy for generation after generation due to the inherited nature of the social structure.

Male spotted hyenas spend a great deal of time forming relationships with the females of the clan. In fact, one of the strategies for gaining favor with the females is to follow them for days or weeks on end. Alpha females prefer to mate with long-tenured males, while young females are more receptive to shorter-tenured males. Males attempt to foster amicable relationships with females to form coalitions and stabilize their position in the social hierarchy. Both males and females mate with multiple members of the opposite sex; however, females secure multiple mating opportunities more frequently. Spotted hyenas would be considered to be polyandrous. Alpha female preference for older males may be an indicator of high male quality. Scientists have found that females rarely mate with immigrant males with tenures of less than two years. Coincidentally, testosterone levels of most immigrants are lower and only increase after they have been part of a new clan for fifteen months. A study done by German scientists Marion East and Heribert Hofer may have found a possible explanation for the testosterone level changes in males: they found that male spotted hyenas queue for status and that their social status increases as their tenure within the social clan increases.[53]

Alpha females breed at a younger age, have greater offspring survival, and reproduce more frequently than lower-ranking females in the clan. Because of the females' dominance and aggressiveness, courting males are extremely wary and take a week to over a month to work up the courage to attempt a mounting. Once the male has worked up the courage, he approaches the female and performs a bowing display with an erect penis. He begins by lowering his muzzle to the ground and then moves forward quickly toward the female before bowing again. After the second bow, the male paws the ground close behind her. If the female is not receptive to the advances of the male, she will growl or lunge or merely stare at him, and he will run.

Due to the unusual anatomy of the female, the male needs to insert his penis vertically into the clitoris. To do this, he must first grab a hold of the female's loins while sliding back on his haunches and partly under her while perilously holding on to her. The male simultaneously rests his head on the female while repeatedly levering up his penis in an attempt to navigate this enlarged clitoris. All the while he is squatting very low on his hind legs to get the right angle while not falling over backward. The copulation can last up to twelve minutes, after which the exhausted male rests his head and body on the female. Upon completion, the pair licks each other's genitals.

Spotted hyenas hunt and capture their own food. They scavenge opportunistically, but no more than any other carnivore. Spotted hyenas occasionally carry out coordinated hunting attacks with the clan but also are successful on their own—one study found that 75 percent of successful hunts were conducted by solo hyenas. A single spotted hyena can take down a wildebeest.

High-ranking female spotted hyenas have first access to food. Prey is usually procured by a single hyena, and then the clan converges on the kill, at which point an intense feeding competition ensues. Once again, social rank determines access to food.

Why have female spotted hyenas evolved to have masculinized genitals? Scientists once thought it was an incidental consequence of high androgen levels, which were selected for through the benefits of aggressive behavior. But scientists Martin Muller and Richard Wrangham proposed an alternative hypothesis: sexual mimicry.[54] They suggested that females imitate male behavior to ward off deadly hostility from same-sex rivals. Muller and Wrangham propose three possible reasons for the female mimicry of males. The camouflage hypothesis could be used as a defense against siblicide, infanticide, and female spotted hyenas killing female rivals. During the first few months of life, male and female cubs are virtually indistinguishable. The authors believe selection could favor females that resemble males and (as a counterstrategy) female ability to discern the sex of their sibling because female cubs kill and assault their sisters more frequently than their brothers. Muller and Wrangham suggest that female spotted hyena genital masculinization constitutes the culmination of a female replication of a male arms race, favored by a tendency for females to direct more severe aggressiveness toward females than males.

As we have seen, there are some clear disadvantages to females mimicking male genitalia. Due to the odd reproductive anatomy, female spotted hyenas lose up to 25 percent of their expected lifetime reproduction, and many first-time mothers die during childbirth. Still, the advantages for female spotted hyenas being at the top of the social hierarchy and being larger and more aggressive and dominant than the males outweigh the disadvantages, as evidenced by the evolution of female spotted hyenas' genitalia.

## HONEYBEES

Honeybees (*Apis mellifera*) are also a female-dominant species with a very unique social structure. Honeybees are native to Africa, Europe, and most of Asia, but they are now found on every continent except Antarctica. Honeybees inhabit many different ecosystems, from semi-wooded areas to grasslands to meadows to gardens. If they can find food, water, and shelter, then hostile environments like wetlands and deserts are also in play.

A honeybee colony is composed of worker bees (which are sterile females), a queen (which is a fertile female), and male bees called drones. Drones do not collect pollen or nectar and do not have stingers. They even need female worker bees to help them eat. The sole role of drones is to mate with the queen. Worker bees (all female bees other than the queen), as the name implies, do all the work. The list of tasks that they perform is remarkable: they clean brood cells, feed larvae and young drones, produce wax, seal honey, feed and groom the queen, build honeycomb, store pollen, coat the walls of the hive with propolis, remove dead bees, fan the hive, carry water, guard the entrance to the hive, and forage and scout for nectar and pollen sources.

The queen honeybee has fully developed reproductive organs and gives birth to virtually all the other bees in the hive. Worker bees select a larva that they feed a special diet so that it will become a sexually mature virgin queen honeybee. If there are other virgin queens in the hive, she will sting, thereby killing any rivals. It is a kill-or-be-killed scenario. The sole surviving queen flies out of the hive to a drone congregation area, where she mates with ten to fifteen drones, which die after mating. The recently inseminated queen stores up to six million sperm in her body and releases them over the course of her life, which can be as long as seven years. A healthy queen is fed a special diet of royal jelly. She can lay roughly 1,000 eggs per day and can control the sex of the eggs that she lays. The queen bee can also release a pheromone that inhibits the workers from starting queen cells.

As the queen gets old, she is replaced through a process called supersedure, during which worker bees cluster tightly around her, raising her temperature, which eventually causes her death.

## THEODORA

Like Black Anna, Theodora is a woman that people should know, and that we do ourselves harm to ignore. Empress of the Byzantine Empire, Theodora (wife of Emperor Justinian) was the embodiment of an alpha female and had a truly remarkable life. The Byzantine Empire was the most powerful force in Europe at the time, and under the reign of Justinian and Theodora, the empire expanded into North Africa and Asia, reaching its greatest size.

Theodora's ascension to power is a legendary story. She was the daughter of a bear trainer in a show that would be similar to a modern-day circus in Constantinople. When her father died, she became an actress and performed in stage shows, some of which were similar to burlesque. After her stage performances, Theodora worked as a courtesan, which was a prostitute for high-ranking clientele such as kings, emperors, ambassadors, and noblemen. Courtesans ranked at the top of the prostitute hierarchy and were usually well educated and well versed in politics.

Justinian was quite smitten with Theodora but was unable to marry her because a law at the time prevented anyone of senatorial rank from marrying an actress. When Justinian took the throne, he changed the law so that he could marry Theodora.

Theodora was a force in her own right; she was active and powerful within the political and cultural framework of her society. While the social structure was very much to her disadvantage, she nevertheless demonstrated the pure dynamism of the feminine in this context. Theodora was a very intelligent woman whom Justinian called his "partner in my deliberations." She helped devise political strategies and advised the emperor on all orders. Theodora also advanced women's rights. Her legislation harshly punished rapists, protected the rights of women going through divorce, expanded property ownership rights, and banned the killing of women who committed adultery. She also set up shelters for former actresses.

But Theodora's biggest moment came in 532 during the Nika riots, which were started by two opposing political parties. One of the factions declared a new emperor to replace Justinian. As the mob set fires to buildings and closed in on Justinian, Theodora, and their inner circle of associates, they prepared to flee. This is when Theodora spoke out and gave a speech to her husband and his advisors that would change history:

My lords, the present occasion is too serious to allow me to follow the convention that a woman should not speak in a man's council. Those whose interests are threatened by extreme danger should think only of the wisest course of action, not of conventions. In my opinion, flight is not the right course, even if it should bring us to safety. It is impossible for a person, having been born into this world, not to die; but for one who has reigned it is intolerable to be fugitive. May I never be deprived of this purple robe, and may I never see the day when those who meet me do not call me empress. If you wish to save yourself, my lord, there is no difficulty. We are rich; over there is the sea, and yonder are the ships. Yet reflect for a moment whether, when you have once escaped to a place of security, you would not gladly exchange such safety for death. As for me, I agree with the adage that the royal purple is the noblest shroud.

Theodora's speech was so influential that it spurned on Justinian and his officers to attack the rioters and put down the rebellion, thus saving the throne (and killing 30,000 people in the process). A remarkable moment from a remarkable woman.

As with Black Anna, the power of Theodora as a symbol today feels complex and twofold. Surely, she represents the power of the feminine both in her ability to respond to and thrive in a social structure that would otherwise work against her—and in the unquestionable efficacy of her leadership. She was not exactly the queen of a matriarchal hive, nor was she a woman disguised as a man, with pseudo-phallic appendages, but she was nevertheless wonderfully compelling in her ability to shape the actions of those around her. Theodora and Black Anna both remain symbols of feminine power that work between those extremes. That is unexpected only to those that close their eyes to the power of womanhood, that read too ambitiously into the narrative that would minimize or ignore the true complexity of the natural world, and to human hierarchies.

## HUMAN ALPHA FEMALES

Anthropologist Monika Sumra defines alpha females as such: "The alpha female is a confident leader who is socially and sexually dominant over others. She is physically strong, more sexually active, and extroverted, and her personality is more masculine than feminine. She believes that men and women are equal and uses collaboration and affiliation strategies to achieve her goals." Dr. Sumra concludes that "contrary to popular narratives, for the study population, the alpha female does not necessarily have sex more frequently than other women, though she is more experienced and enjoys sex more. She does not necessarily make more money or is more educated than other women, and she does not necessarily hold a senior position in her workplace. She reports being strong and extroverted and being aggressive, ambitious, assertive, competitive, and independent, however, not at the expense of being affectionate, gentle, loyal, sensitive to the needs of others, and understanding."[55]

Given Dr. Sumra's definition and analysis of human alpha females, the question still remains: do alpha females and alpha

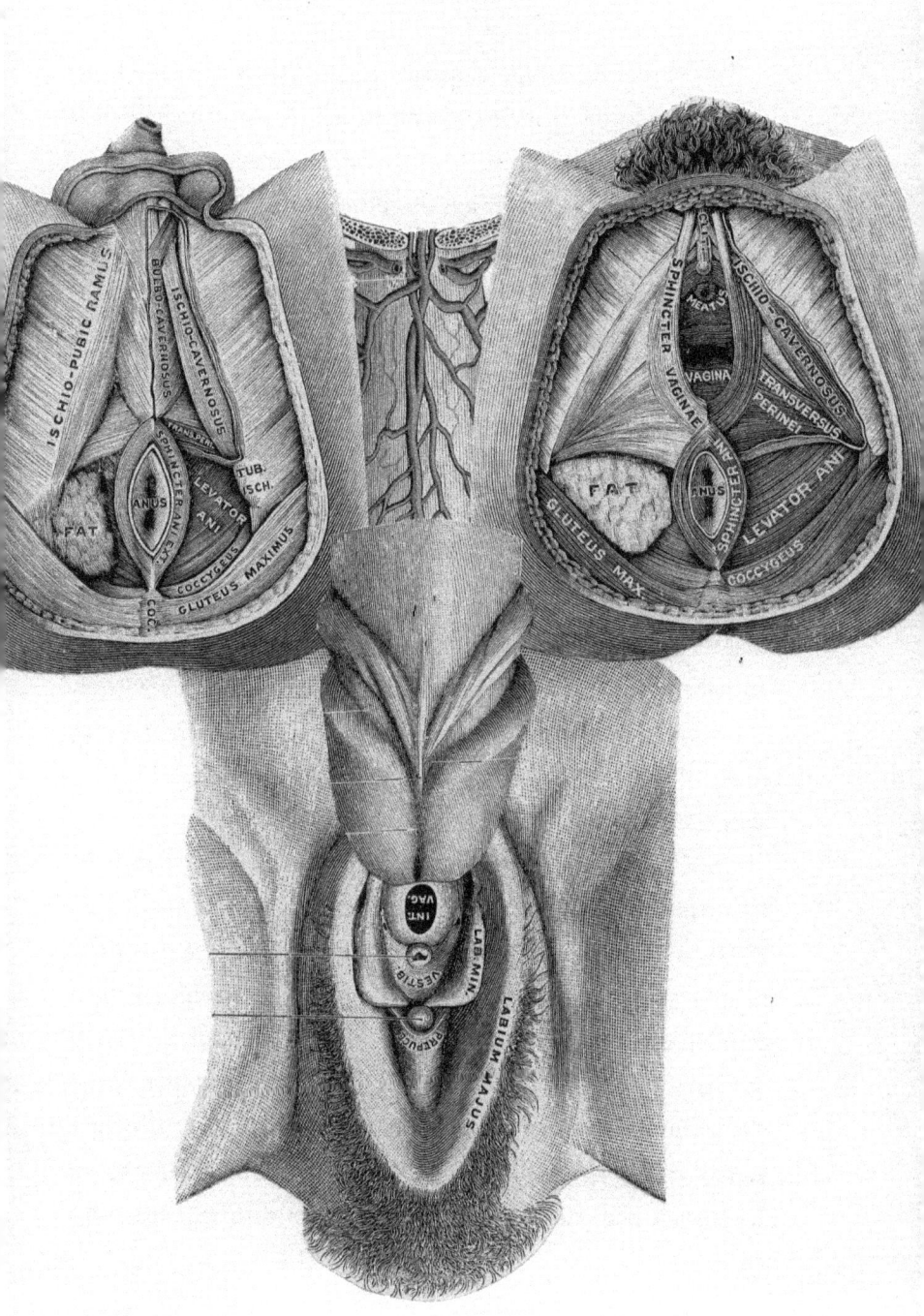

males truly exist in human social groups? I would contend that they may exist but in a very ephemeral and rapidly changing sense that is not so easily defined as with other mammals.

Research conducted by a Swiss professor at the University of Lausanne, Marianne Schmid Mast, revealed that there are some differences in hierarchy formation between males and females.[56] She reviewed and identified three types of social structures: an egalitarian structure where democracy prevails, a crab-basket structure (based on the idea that there is no need for a lid on a basket of crabs because as one tries to climb out, another will pull them back down), and the pecking order (a linear social hierarchy in which one individual dominates over another lower-ranking individual, which repeats itself down the line). Schmid Mast's results showed that women take longer to organize themselves into hierarchies in all-female groups, while men form hierarchies almost immediately. She found that the male hierarchical organization decreases over time, whereas female groups become more organized; however, they both become unstable over longer periods of time.

Both the all-male and the all-female groups exhibited instability in the hierarchies that they initially formed. Schmid Mast's work highlights the complexity found within human social groups. It is interesting to note that although males and females go about forming dominance hierarchies differently, they both end up at the same place. Hierarchies are formed but are subject to rapid change and reorganization. There is an ebb and flow. Human hierarchies change depending on many factors. As Schmid Mast states, "Increasing the knowledge about how hierarchical structures among women develop and what the peculiarities of such hierarchies are in comparison to men can help to optimize work relationships and even inspire new leadership concepts."

## CONCLUSION

As we have seen in this chapter, females have assumed many different roles within social hierarchies across many different species and different points in history. Black Anna was a lower-class woman who shed the nurturing, passive, maternal stereotype and led men into battle—in her dress, at the front of the pack, with her arms outstretched overhead. Pipefish have reversed sex roles, with males caring for the fertilized eggs in their specialized brood pouches and females initiating sexual behavior, complete with sexual ornaments. Spotted hyenas also challenge our understanding of social hierarchies in that females possess a pseudo-penis and are the highest-ranking members of the social hierarchy, while males reside at the bottom of the social structure. Female honeybees perform all the tasks within the colony, while male drones only mate with the queen and die. Honeybees exhibit incredibly complex behaviors and extraordinary levels of sociality. Theodora is an example of a woman who rose from the bottom of the social hierarchy all the way to the top and changed history with her inspirational speech, which spurred a victory in battle.

Power, status, sex, and hierarchy are constantly moving and shifting within the human population and show great variety in the larger animal kingdom. Females across all species show incredible

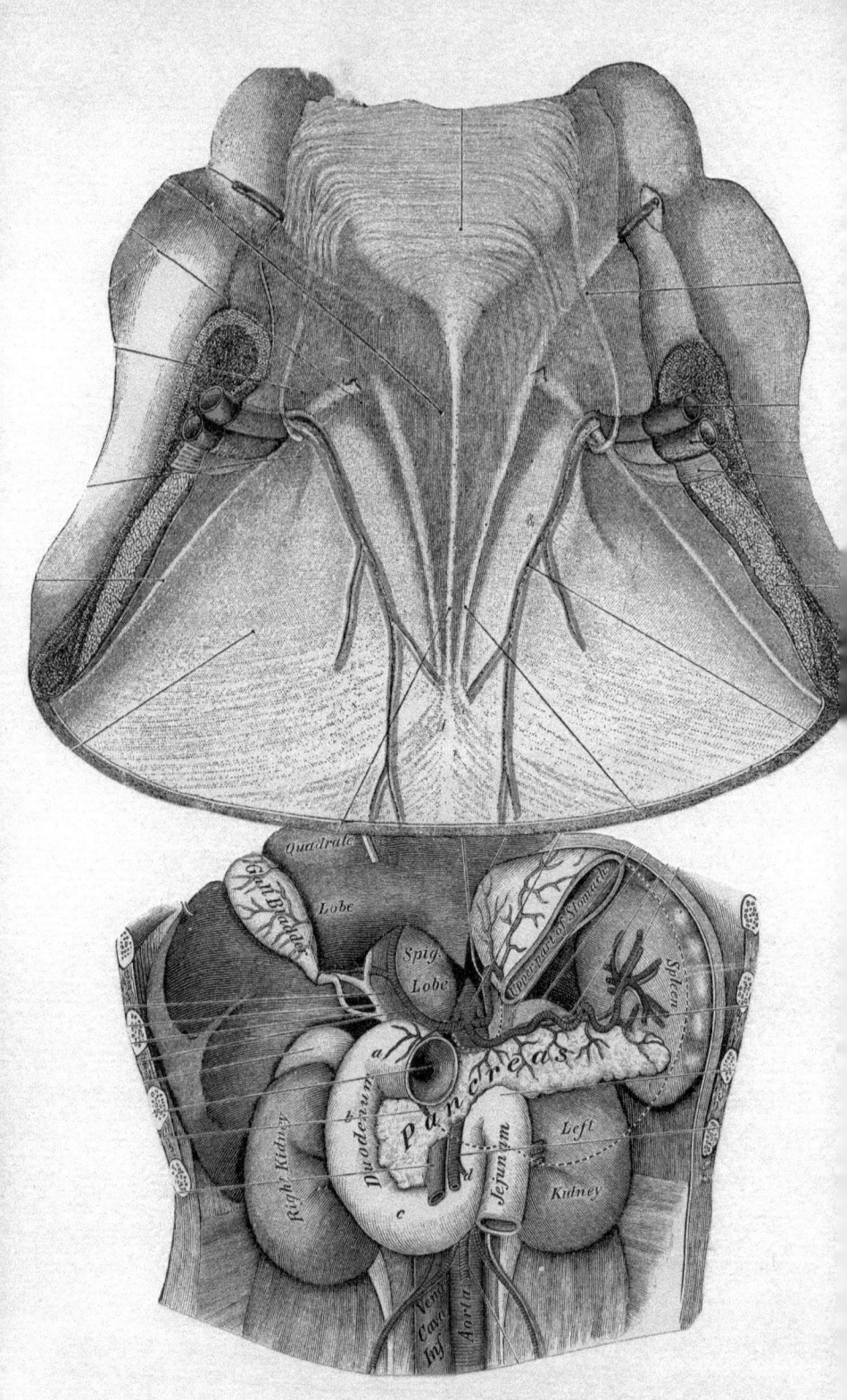

variation when it comes to power, status, sex, and hierarchy. This shows that existing theories, myths, and academic study on the alpha female are incomplete, which has implications for studies that aim to identify or classify women according to a certain female identity.

# PART III
# LOVE AND WAR

# SEVEN
# MORITURI TE SALUTANT

*"If you are extraordinarily sensitive to your surroundings, and your surroundings are extraordinarily frightening, after you have crouched and twitched for a spell, you will eventually send out the serpent. And so the serpent is a Chinese finger trap. There comes a point when you've shoved the mouse down so deep, you can't pull it back. Not without losing a sizeable chunk of who you once were. Look far enough down the throat of the serpent and you'll always find a mouse."*

—DAEMON FAIRLESS

## MAN IN THE ARENA

We all remember the first time that we were punched in the face. It is burned into our memory. Getting punched in the face elicits something deep within our simian brains—something from our evolution.

Getting punched in the face has always meant something, and it always will. It is a message that is hard to deny. The old saying from boxing is that "everyone has a plan until they get hit in the face." It's true: getting hit in the face is a jarring experience. That's why it is so memorable. I remember the first time that I got punched in the face, and I think that I can speak for most people when I say that I did not like it.

Fights always seem to draw a crowd. Some people watch because they are curious; others want to see someone get hurt, while still others are drawn to the spectacle, to the emotion of the moment. The reality is that violence is often ugly, and people frequently get hurt. It can be a scarring experience and can leave people frightened and scared.

Still, professional fighters fight before huge, sold-out crowds in massive stadiums. At one time, horse racing and boxing were the biggest sports in the United States. Now we fill arenas to watch, listen to, and experience everything from sports to music to lectures.

Theodore Roosevelt's often quoted but mis-titled "The Man in the Arena" speech (its actual title is "Citizen in a Republic") is so good that I feel compelled to repeat it once again here:

It is not the critic who counts; not the man who points out how the strong man stumbles, or where the doer of deeds could have done them better. The credit belongs to the man who is actually in the arena, whose face is marred by dust and sweat and blood; who strives valiantly; who errs, who comes short again and again, because there is no effort without error and shortcoming; but who does actually strive to do the deeds; who knows great enthusiasms, the great devotions; who spends himself in a worthy cause; who at the best knows in the end the triumph of high achievement, and who at the worst, if he fails, at least fails while daring greatly, so that his place shall never be with those cold and timid souls who neither know victory nor defeat.

That is some great stuff and, I think, the driving force behind getting people into arenas. As Roosevelt said in yet another speech ("The Strenuous Life"), we admire those who have the guts to step into the arena: "We admire the man who embodies victorious effort; the man who never wrongs his neighbor, who is prompt to help a friend, but who has those virile qualities necessary to win the stern strife of actual life." That is what people want when they go to see a fight, when they go to an athletic event.

Why do individuals fight? It is a straightforward query with a nuanced response. Since the dawn of man, there have been conflicts between people, eliciting a fight-or-flight response. Not every person fights for the same cause. Everyone has a unique perspective and differs from one another. This may lead to breaches between people. The reasons to battle may be love, ego, family, money, power, fear, freedom, sex, sacrifice, or pride. Conflicts between groups of people can be sparked by issues like oppression, politics, race, and culture. Fighting can also be a war with oneself rather than merely a physical conflict with another person. People struggle with their decisions as they try to balance their emotions and logic.

*Homo sapiens* have competed against one another throughout history in sports with survival significance, whether it is javelin throwing, fighting, or wrestling. From an evolutionary perspective, this makes sense because individuals who developed these talents had a higher chance of surviving interpersonal conflict. An outgrowth of that habit is watching combat sports like boxing and wrestling, which provide all the adrenaline without any personal risk. The adrenaline rush that people experience watching fighting and other sports is also known as the fight-or-flight hormone. We get excited when the fighter or team that we're rooting for wins. The brain will release dopamine which makes you feel good. When our preferred fighter or team loses, the brain produces cortisol, which is also known as the stress hormone.

Many people are drawn to fighting, not necessarily for the bloodshed. While athletes in many sports only have their dignity to lose, fighters quite literally risk their bodies and, in some cases, even their lives. The stakes could not be higher; it creates a dramatic spectacle that humans cannot turn away from.

## HAIL EMPEROR

The title of this chapter is "Morituri Te Salutant." It was believed that this phrase was uttered by gladiators as they entered the fighting arena. Translated from Latin, *Morituri te salutant* means "Those who are about to die salute you." The correct phrase is actually *Ave imperator, morituri te salutamus*: "Hail emperor, we who are about to die salute you." Although once believed to be widely used, the phrase seems to have been used rather sparingly. Historians have found that the phrase was documented only twice in Roman history.

The phrase was first used in 52 AD before Emperor Claudius. Before draining the waters of Lake Fucinus, Emperor Claudius decided that he wanted to stage a naval battle there. Nineteen thousand men were used in this naval battle reenactment between Sicilians and Rhodians. The men who were in this battle were not gladiators or professionals with any type of training. They were called the *naumachiarii*, and they were mostly criminals and captives who were condemned to death. These men were desperate to garner the sympathy of the emperor and that is why they uttered the famous phrase *Morituri te salutant*.

Gladiators were professional fighters who competed in front of spectators in ancient Roman amphitheaters such as the Colosseum. According to some historians, the gladiators first appeared in Italy during the time of the Etruscans, who were the Romans' forebears, and gladiators were documented throughout Rome for at least 700 years. Although they were fighters, most of them had been slaves, combat captives, or criminals prior to becoming gladiators.

They were compelled into the role because of their standing. They frequently engaged in battles for their freedom and survival. Gladiatorial combat may have been considered entertainment, but few questioned its brutality.

Some people decided to sign up and become gladiators, as these fights gained prominence because the most powerful and successful gladiators were admired by the general populace. Additionally appealing was the cash they were given for being gladiators.

Gladiators were well trained, regardless of whether they were slaves, convicts, criminals, or gladiators by choice. They resided in a gladiator school (which resembled a barracks) where they trained and improved their abilities. They were usually well-fed because the Romans understood even then that it would improve their strength and fitness. In a similar vein, they got the best medical care.

Gladiator fights were violent contests. Originally, they took place at funerals and as a manner to pay respect to the deceased. As they gained prominence, the governing classes began to host them as a means of amusing the populace and enhancing their own social standing. They were occasionally employed to divert attention away from more troubling social problems.

It was expected at these battles that all combatants would die, although men who displayed courage and bravery were occasionally spared from death.

It's not just humans that fight in arenas, some bird species also fight in arenas like gladiators. Those arenas are called leks, a Swedish word meaning "play," and the bird in question is the greater prairie chicken.

## GREATER PRAIRIE CHICKEN

The darkness of night was just starting to lift and the sky was beginning to turn from black to a translucent gray. The crisp spring air signaled the return of many bird species to their breeding grounds. I was standing in the middle of a lek, the arena in which the alpha males occupy the center position.

Around the perimeter are gathered the lower-ranking males and females. The alpha males fight and dance while the females watch and decide who they want to mate with. These birds return to the same lek year after year. A good location for a lek is a slightly elevated area with no tall trees nearby for predators to perch on.

These sandhills are an eco-region of mixed-grass prairie that stabilizes the sand dunes and supports a tremendous array of plant and animal life. One of the most distinct inhabitants of the region is the greater prairie chicken, a medium-sized bird in the grouse family characterized by rounded wings, black tail feathers, and distinct brown and white body plumage. Males have dark head feathers that they raise up during courtship and orange air sacs on the sides of the neck that they inflate during courtship displays.

In addition to the raised feathers and brightly colored air sacs, males woo females with a complex ritual dance. During this display, males make a deep, hollow sound; for that reason, locals often refer to the area as the booming grounds. Of course, it's not all pageantry. A male's position in the lek determines his mating success, which has, in turn, been determined by his place in the dominance hierarchy. A few alpha males claim the center-most position in any lek, and this announces their breeding potential. A few beta males benefit from their concentric proximity to the prime position in the center.

Each male occupies a little territory within the lek. Lower-ranking or yearling males establish territories around the periphery of the lek. Younger males bide their time, waiting for vacancies to appear in the more optimal territories toward the center of the arena.

For the most part, territories are relatively stable within each season and from one year to the next; however, fights can occur both over physical boundaries within the lek and for social position within the hierarchy. Fights often start as calls but often escalate into physical confrontation with striking and pulling of feathers with their wings, beaks, and feet. Position within the lek is of paramount importance because the top-ranking males will obtain the overwhelming majority of the copulations.

Females are keen observers of what happens within the lek. As females approach and watch from the periphery, they choose which male they would like to mate with from the display group based on the male's fitness, courtship display, and fighting ability. After mating, females fly away from the lek to nest and rear the young alone.

### SHARP-TAILED GROUSE

Sharp-tailed grouse also inhabit these prairies. Native Americans called sharp-tailed grouse the fire bird because of its reliance on naturally occurring prairie fire to keep its habitat open and ideally situated.

Sharp-tailed grouse are entirely dependent on this open-grassland habitat for survival. The setting of their lek requires a minimum of an eighth-mile diameter free of woody vegetation, and the grouse are completely intolerant of any conifers within a quarter mile of the lek, as these trees would be ideal spots for ambitious predators. The terrain of the lek is usually flat or slightly convex and free of trees.

Eight to twelve birds arrive on the lek about forty-five minutes before sunrise and perform for the next three to four hours. Males perform an elaborate dance during which their head and neck feathers are raised and tail feathers are fanned out and vibrated sideways. Males also stamp their feet rapidly while spreading their wings with their tips curved downward. They inflate their purple neck sacs and hoot or coo for the attention of the hens, which are congregated around the edge of the lek, enjoying the performance as they select a male for mating.

Fights occur occasionally on the lek when lower-ranking males challenge the dominant males. These fights can be vicious, with one male finally submitting by fleeing the scene. Body size and fitness are important determinants in these fights involving territory acquisition and maintenance on the lek.

As we have seen, humans fight in arenas, while birds such as the greater prairie chicken and the sharp-tailed grouse fight in leks. Oddly enough, there is also a reptile that fights and displays in a lek, the marine iguana.

## MARINE IGUANAS

The Galapagos Islands hold a special place in the hearts and minds of most biologists. The islands were made famous by Charles Darwin and have become a natural laboratory for studying evolution. I was fortunate enough to visit the islands in the mid-1990s. I distinctly remember seeing marine iguanas sunning themselves on the volcanic rock and excreting salt crystals from their nasal glands (which they do to rid themselves of excess salt from consuming marine algae). It is an experience unlike any other, something truly remarkable to witness.

Marine iguanas (*Amblyrhynchus cristatus*) feed primarily on marine algae, which is found in the cold ocean waters. This presents a dilemma: how to regulate their body temperatures when physiologically, they are incapable of doing so. They are forced to use the radiant energy of the sun to warm up. Marine iguanas are especially vulnerable to predation when their body temperatures are low because it affects their mobility. To compensate for their lack of movement, they become very aggressive, lunging and biting.

Male marine iguanas are quite a bit longer and weigh twice as much as females. Females reach sexual maturity by the age of three to five years, while males reach sexual maturity at the age of six to eight years. Males begin to establish their territories within the lek several months before the mating season (which is December through March). Large males defend mating territories during the breeding season for up to three months. The territories of the male iguanas are often clustered near to one another and vary in size from one to forty square meters.

Smaller males occasionally challenge larger males. When a medium-sized or smaller male challenges a larger male in the lek, he begins by bobbing his head while opening his mouth. He also adopts a stiff walking posture and raises the crest on his head and back. If the challenge is accepted, they essentially engage in a headbutting contest that can last for hours. The combative males are rarely injured during these contests, but there are still winners and losers.

Females prefer to mate with larger males. Females also assess the males' head bobbing, the quality of the territory, pheromones, and the location of the territory within the lek. Males have greater mating success when their territory is near the center of the lek. Once again males use a variety of reproductive strategies. Large, territorial males use head bobbing and positioning within the lek to gain copulation attempts, while marginal males physically pursue females outside of their territories, hoping to bite and mount them. Sneaker males attempt to mate with females when the large territorial males are distracted with fighting or copulating.

Martin Wikelski studied marine iguanas and found that smaller males increase their reproductive success when the lek is larger in size. "Lekking in marine iguanas, therefore, may represent a 'hotshot' phenomenon where small territorial males associate with large males to increase reproductive success."[57]

The hotshot model hypothesis postulates that attractive males, also known as hotshots, draw the attention of both males and females. Females seek out these hotshots because they are attracted to them, while males seek out the hotshots in hopes of gaining copulations due to their proximity to the more attractive males. Wikelski found that although females preferred to mate with the large territorial males, the smaller territorial males "got some accidental matings."

## THE HOTSHOT PHENOMENON AND HUMAN HIERARCHIES

Can the hotshot phenomenon be applied to humans? I would say yes. If we look at bands or professional sports teams, the most attractive males draw the attention of both males and females for different reasons. The males congregate around the attractive male hoping to interact with the females who are attracted to the hotshot. Females are hoping to land the attractive male, while the other males are hoping to "pick up his scraps."

Hierarchies exist not only within leks but also at dinner tables. Many families have prescribed seating arrangements based on unspoken hierarchies, especially during the holidays. Positioning within the lek is quite important, as is often the case with seating arrangements at dinners, weddings, parties, and work functions.

Hierarchies exist in almost all human interactions. They exist in our families, friendships, workplaces, sports teams, places of worship, military, government, book clubs, and poker groups. Hierarchies can be useful—perhaps even helpful—but they have also been used for horrible purposes to subjugate and maim or kill our fellow human beings. Atrocities against humanity and the

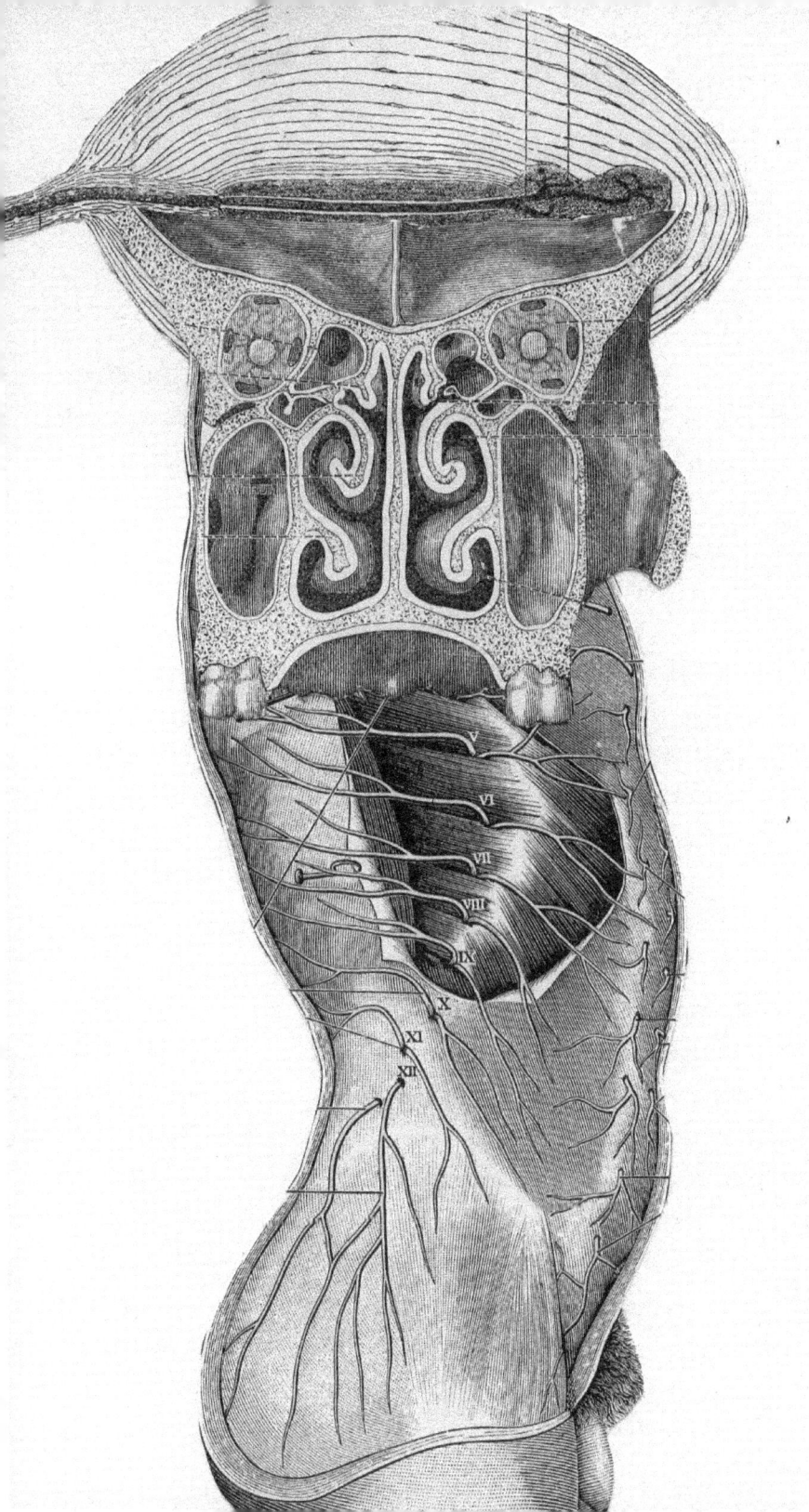

natural world have also spawned from hierarchies. A watchful eye must be kept on hierarchy formation and continuation so as to not veer toward nefarious purposes.

Most of the time we are unaware of the hierarchies through which we move on a daily basis. I doubt most of us think about it when we are with our families or around our friends. Social hierarchies change frequently among humans. They can be quite fluid and dynamic.

Cultural anthropologist Christopher Boehm, author of *Hierarchy in the Forest*, made the argument that "humans have an innate tendency to dominate as well as an innate tendency to resent being dominated."[58] Authors Daniel Bell and Wang Pei stated, "Hierarchy is a ubiquitous feature of human relations, and it is unrealistic to wish it away. That's not to say we can't have the equality of friendship, but any social relation also needs to make room for hierarchy, and the task is to distinguish between good and bad forms of hierarchy and to promote social relations that have more of the former."[59]

Human social hierarchies exist much like leks: to display social dominance that, in some cases, ultimately results in propagating the species. That may be through greater mating opportunities, like we see with the hotshot phenomenon, or it may be through more psychological or emotional gains.

Humans also have another way to the top of a social group. Professors Joseph Henrich and Francisco Gil-White propose the "information goods" theory, where prestige becomes the currency by which hierarchies are formed.[60] Many species, including humans, have typically used traditional dominance-based (with force or the threat of force) interactions to further their position in the hierarchy. The prestige-based hierarchy advanced by Henrich and Gil-White suggests that people who are seen as skilled or competent are granted privileged places in society, and lower-status people voluntarily defer to them so they can continue to learn from these skilled, high-status individuals. In a prestige-based hierarchy, a low-status person should approach the high-status individual, try to get close to them, and keep an eye on them. This will increase the likelihood that the low-status actor will be able to learn from the high-status actor. This is in direct contrast to a dominance-based hierarchy, in which a low-ranking individual avoids contact with a higher-ranking member by moving away and maintaining a distance.

## CONCLUSION

We are drawn to arenas for the spectacle, to see the gladiatorial spirit in action. We can also see the importance of competition. Not all competition is bad; sometimes it is good to compete. Females watch what is going on inside arenas as well as behaviors outside of arenas to make decisions on who they might want to mate with. Female choice drives much of sexual selection.

Location matters. Position within an arena/lek matters greatly. If an individual is not happy with their position in a social hierarchy, they could try ascribing to the hotshot phenomenon, also known as the hotspot hypothesis.

For a person who is not interested in fighting, arenas, or traditional dominance hierarchies, I would suggest ascribing to the prestige-based hierarchical model as a way to improve one's status. People seek out and respect highly competent people in exchange for access to learning through copying. The development of direct social learning abilities in human ancestry has led to the development of prestige.

As much as I have talked about fighting and arenas among birds, reptiles, and humans, I think the take-home lesson is that ultimately, we are locked in a profound battle with ourselves. The question becomes: How do we win in the arena with only one opponent staring back at us in the mirror? How do we overcome our own fears and insecurities to be successful in life? This is ultimately where all battles are won and lost. Step toward the things that we are afraid of because that is the enemy that can cause the most harm.

# EIGHT
# A CALL TO ARMS

> "Earth! render back from out thy breast
> A remnant of our Spartan dead!
> Of the three hundred grant but three,
> To make a new Thermopylae."
> —GEORGE NOEL GORDON, LORD BYRON

## ROCKY

The movie *Rocky* is a worldwide cultural phenomenon. People around the world know and like the fictional character Rocky Balboa. The movie embodies many themes that people relate to and admire about the human condition: it is about the underdog, determination, failure, success, love, hardship, luck, overcoming adversity—and fighting.

Fighting is one of the most primal things that humans engage in. Fighting, in many ways, is "pure." It matters little where you went to school, where you grew up, who your parents are, how much or how little money you may have, how intelligent you are, what you look like, how you speak, or what nation you live in. It is, in some ways, the ultimate equalizer. Are there ways to make a fight unequal and unfair? Of course, but at its core, a fight strips away much of the noise. Humans have been fighting for as long as we have inhabited the earth. We are an incredibly intelligent species, yet we still fight. Our evolutionary ancestors such as *Australopithecus anamensis*, *Homo habilis*, and *Homo neanderthalensis* all fought. To some extent, fighting may be embedded in our DNA.

Our fellow great apes fight. Aggression and violence is well documented in male chimpanzees, gorillas, and orangutans. Human males also fight frequently. Recent studies have even shown that the physiology of the male body is designed for punching power. The ability of humans to form a fist is used against others as a weapon.

Fighting in humans and our great ape ancestors probably evolved via sexual selection and male-male competition. Strength and weapon use also probably evolved in defense against predators.

The ability to fight, however, does not guarantee victory. In the movie, Rocky lost the fight but he went the distance against the champion. As obsessed as our culture is with winners, it is ironic that we love, in this case, the loser. Somehow the movie transcends winning and losing.

## THE BATTLE OF THERMOPYLAE

The same holds true with the Battle of Thermopylae. Although the Greeks lost the battle, it is still remembered in many ways to be a victory. The Battle of Thermopylae occurred in 480 BC when Xerxes I, the king of Persia, invaded Greece, looking to expand his territory and continue what his father Darius had started. The Spartans used the topography of their country to their advantage. As Xerxes invaded Greece and started moving south, his army had to go through the narrow pass of Thermopylae. Leonidas I of Sparta positioned his small army at this narrow pass to gain an advantage. Xerxes's army was estimated to be anywhere from 70,000 to 300,000 men, while Leonidas commanded an army of only 7,000 men. Despite the immense disparity in numbers, the Greeks were able to hold the pass and inflict considerable damage to the Persian forces. On the second day of the battle, a local shepherd offered to show the Persians a mountain path to attack the Greeks from behind on the other end of the pass. This sealed the fate of the Greeks. Upon learning of the Persian army's movement, Leonidas sent most of his men away. The final battle featured only 300 Spartans and roughly 1,000 other combatants fighting against Xerxes's massive army. All of them were killed, including Leonidas.

Why are humans drawn to stories such as this, where a vastly outnumbered army fights a colossal force to the death? It awakens something in our primal lizard brain. The ideals of sacrifice and bravery in the face of sure death is something that humans respect and I think, on some level, envy. We envy those individuals who have the courage to stand up and fight. We wish to be the fighter; we envy their heroism but not their folly.

In the rest of the animal kingdom, we may not find such outward sentimentality over fights to the death, but we do find fighting—a lot of it. Our animal brethren are battling it out for love, territory, power, and every other reason under the sun. Sometimes, as we will see, might does make right, but don't discount the underdogs just yet.

## BIGHORN SHEEP

Bighorn sheep (*Ovis canadensis*) use weapons to combat their rivals. They are found in the Rocky Mountains, from Canada down through Colorado. Depending on the season, they live at elevations of 800–2,500 meters. As with many mammals, males (119–127 kilograms) are larger than females (53–91 kilograms). Their winter coat is gray, while their summer coat is brown.

As their name implies, bighorn sheep, especially the males, have big horns. Their skull morphology and associated anatomy have evolved to support such apparatus. They have double-layered skulls supported by an additional framework of bone to protect the brain while doing battle, and the skull is connected to the spine by a giant tendon that helps absorb the blows from the collisions. A male's horns may weigh as much as fourteen kilograms, and his status in the hierarchy is determined by horn size and age.

The head-to-head combat between males can attain epic proportions, lasting upward of twenty hours, with males reaching speeds of up to twenty miles per hour. These collisions are no joke; they echo among the mountains.

Males fight for access to females, and the competition is intense and violent. Generally only males that are seven and older are able to compete and mate. Scientists Fanie Pelletier, John Hogg, and Marco Festa-Bianchet speculate this is because males of this age switch their mating strategy from the costly coursing strategy to the less costly and more successful tactic of tending.[61] The breeding or rutting season is in the fall and early winter. Births occur in the spring, with the males absent from parental care.

Alpha males are the largest both in terms of body size and horn size. Although the high-ranking, dominant males have greater mating success, as we have seen with other species, lower-ranking males find alternative ways to sire young. Younger, smaller rams employ two alternative mating tactics called coursing and blocking. Coursing occurs when subordinate rams try to mate with a female that is being attended to by a dominant male. It is a high-risk but also a high-gain strategy.

Even if the subordinate ram is successful, ewes resist their advances. Scientist John Hogg has documented the great lengths that females will go to avoid copulating with subordinate males: "Ewes resist rams attempting coursing copulations by accelerating, dodging or whirling as a coursing ram tries to mount, perching on ledges that are difficult to approach, standing under rock overhangs or deadfalls, and winding through aspen groves or other vegetation that limits male maneuvers."[62] These females go to extreme lengths to avoid these "victorious" males. But we know through paternity testing that these coursing males are successful. Hogg postulates that the development of concussive rather than penetrating weaponry has made fighting less dangerous and possibly more energetically cost-effective.

The other mating tactic that subordinate males use is called blocking, which is when a subordinate ram prevents females from entering the tending area They block the females from getting to the alphas and attempt to sequester the ewes until they become receptive to the lower-ranking males.

Both blocking and especially coursing rely on endurance, agility, and speed, whereas tending is the domain of big and strong males.

The most successful tactic is the one employed by the alpha males, called tending. Tending occurs when the highest ranking ram defends a single estrous ewe. The male will stay with the female for up to two days, courting her and copulating with her repeatedly during this time. Dominant males not only use their horned weaponry to fend off and fight lower-ranking males, but they also engage in ritualized battles with other males. Mass is the name of the game for high-ranking males. Larger body size and weight along with massive horns determine dominance rank among male bighorn sheep.

## RUSTY CRAYFISH

Crayfish are another species that uses weaponry and size to determine rank within the hierarchy. Crayfish look like tiny lobsters. They inhabit lakes, streams, and ponds, preferably with a rocky substrate or debris that they can use for cover. Rusty crayfish (*Orconectes rusticus*) are found throughout the Great Lakes region as well as the East Coast, from New York up through New England.

Rusty crayfish mate during three of the four seasons: early spring, late summer, or early fall. Fertilized eggs are attached to swimmerets located underneath the female's abdomen. Crayfish eggs hatch in three to six weeks, depending on the temperature of the water. The young juveniles stay attached to their mother's swimmerets for several weeks before venturing out on their own.

Rusty crayfish have a lifespan of three to four years. They feed on a wide variety of foods, including plants, snails, insects, and fish eggs. Rusty crayfish excavate shallow burrows under rocks or debris. They are aggressive toward other species of crayfish and predatory fish, assuming a position with their claws raised. Rusty crayfish are also aggressive toward other rusty crayfish. When they cross paths, they elevate their bodies high on their legs and raise their claws high to appear as big as possible. This is called the meral spread. After the meral spread, the crayfish begin to wrestle, at first without their claws, but eventually things escalate and the claws come out.

In addition to weapon (claw) use, rusty crayfish also use chemical signals to communicate. The stronger the urine odor, the shorter and more passive the fight. Urine scents are also used to recognize victors and losers from previous antagonistic encounters. If two crayfish have fought before, the crayfish that won the first fight will recognize that same opponent and use dominance displays before engaging in a second (shorter) encounter with this individual.

Fighting strategies differ among males depending on their physical size and the size of their claws. Some crayfish back down after the meral spread and move on. If neither opponent backs down, the situation may escalate to fighting. Since larger rusty crayfish have larger, potentially more dangerous claws, larger males are slower to escalate the fight, and they fight more conservatively. This assessment of an opponent's relative fighting ability prior to engaging in combat actually occurs in a wide variety of animals, including humans. This is valuable information to acquire since it can provide feedback on whether to initiate, escalate, retaliate, or retreat.

Researchers Lisa Schroeder and Robert Huber found that small crayfish were quick to escalate fights, while larger-sized and larger-clawed rusty crayfish took a more measured approach, assessing the opponent's strength before fights progressed to the next level.[63] Small crayfish with small claws present a lesser chance for injury incurred from the smaller weapons. As such, smaller crayfish are more likely to throw caution to the wind and escalate conflicts with higher intensities and much more rapidly overall than the larger crayfish. Small crayfish with small weapons are also more vulnerable to predation. Losing a claw to predation or fighting is devastating because it is needed to defend against predators, to fight against other crayfish, and for reproduction.

Males possessing larger claws dominate over smaller-clawed males during intermale conflicts. The work of scientist W. Andy Snedden revealed that large-clawed males are better able to secure and position females for copulation. He also documented that large-clawed males copulate for longer periods of time in comparison to smaller-clawed males.

## HORNED BEETLE

Insects also use weapons in hierarchy formation. The horned beetle (*Onthophagus acuminatus*), also known as a dung beetle because it feeds on feces, is found in the rainforests of Central America.

Horned beetles are sexually dimorphic, with males usually possessing horns while females rarely have horns. Males have two horns at the base of their head. The horns are used in intrasexual combat for access to females. There is also dimorphism within just male horned beetles. Some males have large horns, while others have small horns or no horns at all. This is usually associated with the physical size of the male.

Horned beetles' strength-to-weight ratio makes them one of the strongest organisms on the planet. Small beetles are able to invest more energy into growing strong exoskeletons, which are better for bearing weight versus animals with soft tissue. The strength of horned beetles is used to maneuver their food, dig tunnels, and fight in head-to-head battles both above and below ground.

Once again, different mating strategies have emerged depending on the size of the males. Large males employ a tactic called guarding, where they attempt to restrict access to females deeper in the tunnel. Guarding males fight off intruding males should they enter the tunnel, and they also post up at the entrance to the tunnel to ward off rival males. These horned males also walk the length of the tunnel on patrol. Douglas Emlen has studied these beetles for many years and has described the male–male conflict as such: "Rival males could gain possession of a tunnel only by forcibly evicting the resident male, and both fights and turnovers were frequent. Fights over tunnel occupancy entailed repeated butting, wrestling and pushing of opponents, and fights continued until one of the contestants left the tunnel."[64]

Lower-ranking males employ a different tactic entirely. Since they do not have horns to fight with (or have horns that are so rudimentary that they avoid conflict entirely), they use the sneaking method, attempting to bypass the higher-ranking guarding males. The hornless males dig a side tunnel near the guarded tunnel. They dig down below where the guarding male is in the tunnel and then turn horizontally into the main tunnel. The sneaker male is then able to enter the tunnel undetected and mate with the female.

Another method that the hornless males use is to enter the guarded tunnel directly, either when the horned male was feeding or off to the side. If successful, the sneaker males exit the tunnels immediately after mating. The sneaker males are frequently caught and evicted before they reach the female, but many hornless males are successful with side tunnels and sneaking in guarded tunnels. As Emlen observed, "Females appeared to mate with hornless males just as readily as with horned males. No female ever rejected mating with any male, and copulation durations were not different for horned and hornless males. These results are consistent with a mating system characterized by intense inter-male competition over access to females, and where smaller, competitively inferior males adopt a non-aggressive behavioral alternative to encounter females."

Why don't small males have horns? Emlen proposed that large horns may be an impediment to moving rapidly through tunnels, or horn production may be energetically costly, with smaller, hornless males allocating those resources elsewhere. Emlen's research has also uncovered that "males with relatively longer horns developed with significantly smaller eyes than males with relatively shorter horns." So smaller males are able to move faster and more efficiently through tunnels without horns and with better eyesight.

Scientists believe that dung beetles have evolved brawn because strength is often the determining factor in head-to-head combat with other males. Large body size and strength are two factors that can determine the victor in fights, but the main characteristic in winning physical competitions is horn length. The large males with longer horns win fights and thereby win access to females.

## HUMAN SIZE AND WEAPONS

In humans, males are about 15 percent heavier than females and six inches taller. The average male in the United States weighs 190 pounds (86 kg) and is 5'9" tall (175 cm), while the average female in the United States weighs 163 pounds (74 kg) and is 5'4" (162 cm).

Why are males generally larger than females? The most common answer to this question is that males compete through physical fighting for access to females so sexual selection has led to men being larger than women. Women are saddled with producing

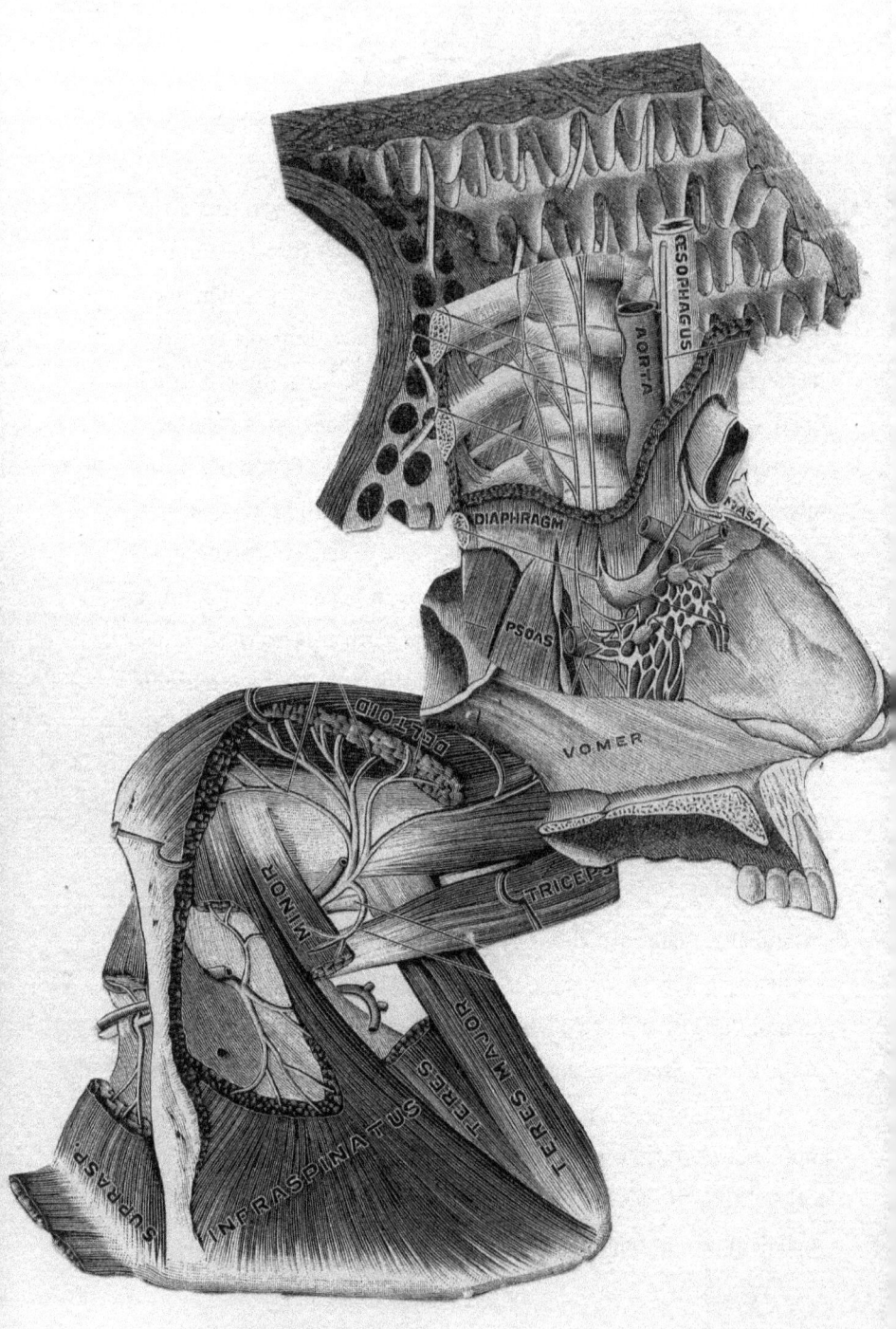

eggs, which are big and expensive to produce, while sperm is cheap. Females are also encumbered for several years with pregnancy, childbirth, and childrearing, meaning females invest more in reproduction, while men invest more in muscles.

The sexual selection and male competition explanation for dimorphism has been challenged by some competing ideas. The first theory comes from French anthropologists Priscille Touraille and Pierre-Henri Gouyon, who state that natural selection should also favor larger females because their probability of dying while giving birth is reduced.[65] Yet in practically all known communities worldwide, limits are frequently targeted at the crucial stage of a woman's reproductive existence, and women as a group are expected to eat less food in terms of quantity and quality than men do (which might explain dimorphism between the sexes).

Why do food taboos exist, and why do they disproportionately affect women and children? One explanation may be that in some cultures, men may declare meat and other delicacies off limits to others for solely egoistic motives. Scientist Daniel Fessler suggests that females worldwide eat less food when they are ovulating because of increased time dedicated to mate seeking or mating activities.[66] As is the case in most mammals, females who spend the most time mating during the viable window have the highest chance of becoming pregnant.

Yet another factor limiting female caloric intake is that in many traditional societies there are food taboos surrounding special occasions that involve female bodily functions, such as pregnancy, menstruation, giving birth, and breastfeeding. Food taboos are societal conventions that impact people throughout the world to varying degrees based on their gender, religion, and culture. They may serve as a way to conserve resources and protect one's health, or they may help groups stay cohesive, supporting a group in maintaining its identity in the face of outsiders and thus fostering a sense of belonging.

Another competing hypothesis to male competition is the effect of estrogen on bone growth. Biological anthropologist Holly Dunsworth has explored estrogen and bone development and states that estrogen stimulates long bone growth.[67] The ovaries bump up estrogen production during puberty, which in turn stimulates the growth plates in the bones, causing the bones to lengthen. This is why during early adolescence, girls are usually taller than boys. The height advantage is short-lived however, as Dunsworth explains the high levels of estrogen make the growth plates fuse, effectively stopping the lengthening of bones. The bones in men continue to grow for several more years "until their estrogen peaks, so they end up taller." The research of clinical professor in pediatrics Karen Klein has found that estrogen peaks in boys five years after puberty begins.

Regardless of why men are larger than women, it is common to find men who take pride in their size. Having worked in construction for the past thirty years, I have witnessed a constant appraisal of muscle mass, or lack thereof, on jobsites. One morning, I was just getting my day started at the site when I came across a laborer who said, "What happened to your biceps? You need to work out. Your forearms look big, but you need bigger biceps." I believe this type of mentality also stretches into other jobs, but perhaps not with the same prevalence or intensity as within the field of construction.

Why do males generally have more muscle mass than females? Is it based on resources or nutrition? Does it have something to do with estrogen and bone growth? Did greater physical strength in males evolve to fight against other males over access to females? Did male strength evolve from weapon use in defense against predators? These are all interesting questions with compelling answers, but I think that it is a combination of these factors that caused the muscle mass and strength differential among males and females, with sexual selection being the main driver.

Males are, on average, 60–70 percent stronger in the upper body and 30–40 percent stronger in the lower body than females. Research coming out of the University of Utah suggests that the upper body of human males may be specialized for physical combat with rival males. Specifically upper arm strength, which translates into powerful punches.

## CONCLUSION

The male body has evolved to fight against other males, usually by throwing fists at one another. As we have seen in species as varied as bighorn sheep, rusty crayfish, and horned beetles, males fight for access to females through physical combat using horns, claws, and fists. Males across species fight, but males across species have also found alternative ways to be successful without fighting. Among bighorn sheep, there are many ways for individuals of all shapes and sizes to be successful; one does not have to be a victorious fighter to have success. With rusty crayfish, fighting strategies change based on the size of the individual, and physical confrontations have consequences. For horned beetles, weapons and fighting are not always the best solution, as smaller horned beetles do not have horns but are faster and can see better than their larger counterparts. Throwing punches is not the only way to win the woman.

## NINE
# SNEAKY FUCKERS

"Kya dropped the journal on her lap, her mind drifting with the clouds. Some female insects eat their mates, overstressed mammal mothers abandon their young, many males design risky or shifty ways to outsperm their competitors. Nothing seemed too indecorous as long as the tick and the tock of life carried on. She knew this was not a dark side to Nature, just inventive ways to endure against all odds. Surely for humans there was more."

—DELIA OWENS

## THE MILLER'S TALE

Evolutionary biologist John Maynard Smith coined the phrase "sneaky fuckers." A sneaky fucker is a subordinate male that employs a strategy in which he tries to take advantage of opportunities to mate with females when the dominant male is occupied, thereby leading to his reproductive success. This is also known as *kleptogamy*, as defined by the Oxford Dictionary of Psychology: "a behavior pattern in which males from outside a group, or lacking status within the group, attempt to mate with females from the group, often by means of some deceptive behavior."[68] The word *kleptogamy* has its origins in the Greek language, *klepto* (to steal) and *gamos* (marriage). This leads me to Chaucer's *Canterbury Tales*, specifically "The Miller's Tale."

"The Miller's Tale" is a story about a carpenter and his wife and two other men. John, the carpenter, is married to a beautiful younger woman named Alisoun. In order to supplement his income, John rents out a room to a local university student named Nicholas. Nicholas takes an immediate interest in Alisoun, but he is not the only one who has his eyes on her. Absolon, the effeminate parish clerk in town, also fancies Alisoun.

One day John heads into town, and while he is away, Nicholas makes his move. Nicholas grabs Alisoun "by the queynte" and states, "Love me all-at-once or I shall die." She initially resists, at which point he starts to cry. After a short while, they hatch a plan to carry out their affair and fool her jealous husband.

Soon after beginning her affair with Nicholas, Alisoun attends church, where Absolon tries to woo her by singing love songs outside her window and giving her gifts. Alisoun is not interested in Absolon and rejects his advances. She and Nicholas return to their scheme to fool her husband and consummate their relationship.

Nicholas tells John that their town will be visited upon by a flood of biblical proportions as told to him by God. He convinces the carpenter to build individual wood tubs to be hung from the ceiling of the barn. As the flood water rises, they can cut the ropes holding the tubs and float safely away from danger. John loads each tub with provisions and an ax to cut the rope if necessary. Then John, Alisoun, and Nicholas all climb up the ladders into their respective tubs. As soon as they sense that John has fallen asleep, Alisoun and Nicholas descend and go and sleep together in John's bed.

That same evening, the eager Absolon returns to Alisoun's window pleading for a kiss. Instead of offering her lips, when Absolon closes his eyes and leans in for a kiss, she sticks her naked behind out, and he kisses her ass. Embarrassed and angry, he leaves, listening to the two of them laughing at him. Absolon runs off to the blacksmith to grab a red-hot poker. He returns to the window offering a golden ring in return for one kiss. This time Nicholas wants to get in on the fun, so he sticks his ass out of the window and farts in Absolon's face. Absolon quickly regroups and shoves the red-hot poker into Nicholas's ass.

Nicholas immediately howls in pain, yelling "Water, water, water!" John is roused from his sleep and, hearing the cries for water, assumes there is a flood. He cuts the rope securing his tub to the rafters, and it comes crashing down to the ground, breaking his arm in the process. The ruckus attracts the neighbors, who laugh at John's folly.

I think this story embodies the sneaky fucker strategy. Here you have several males pursuing a female who is already married, using cunning, clever, deceptive behavior. Both Nicholas and Absolon chase after Alisoun using subterfuge, trickery, and deception; they are sneaky fuckers.

Now let's explore some other species that exhibit sneaky fucker behavior.

## OCTOPUSES

Male octopuses also exhibit sneaky fucker behavior. The algae octopus (*Abdopus aculeatus*) is found off of the coasts of Indonesia, the Philippines, and Australia. This octopus is so named because its camouflage resembles algae. The algae octopus is small, with its body about the size of a tennis ball and its legs measuring about twenty-five centimeters in length.

This octopus is unique in that it often leaves the water, moving from one tidal pool to the next, when hunting for food. The algae octopus inhabits areas that are primarily covered in sea grass and takes shelter in dens dug into the sandy seabed. It typically feeds on crabs, often capturing its prey by jetting forward. Once the octopus has secured its prey, it uses its beak to get through the crab's hard exoskeleton.

Octopuses have well-developed nervous systems, are exceptional learners/problem-solvers, and are very visual animals. The algae octopus also exhibits a complex mating system, utilizing four distinct mating strategies. When a large male algae octopus occupies a den adjacent to a female's, the male extends his hectocotylus (mating arm) all the way into the female's den. The pair mates repeatedly over the course of a week. This tactic is known as adjacent guarding.

During adjacent guarding, the female may be responsive to mating attempts from sneaker males as well. A sneaker male is smaller in size and is opportunistic in his mating attempts. The sneaker waits until the guarding male is distracted or away feeding to approach the female. He usually approaches the female's den in a way that the guarding male cannot see him, often using obstructions for cover. Sometimes he also camouflages himself to look like a female. If he successfully reaches the female's den without her rebuffing his copulation attempt, he will mate for a longer duration than other males. Scientists do not know why but speculate that they might be transferring additional sperm or removing a rival's sperm.

Another mating behavior exhibited by males is the transient mating tactic, in which a male will mate with a smaller, opportunistic female that he encounters while out foraging for food. The females that these transient males mate with are generally smaller than the guarded females. In this mating behavior, the males depart the mating area shortly after the final withdrawal of the hectocotylus, as they are not concerned with guarding the females.

The final mating tactic observed in the algae octopus is called temporary guarding. This occurs when a male–female pair temporarily enters into a guarding situation after the male attempts to mate with the female at the den or while she looks for food. Temporarily guarding males fight off rival males using aggressive behaviors such as chasing and grappling. Both adjacent and temporary mate guarding are crucial and effective strategies utilized by males to monopolize females who appear to be unselective.

Male–male aggression and competition for mates is common in algae octopuses. Larger males are generally the victors over smaller males. Behaviors found in fighting males include chasing, whipping of arms, and grappling. One scientist recorded a truly remarkable occurrence where a male was able to fend off a rival male while still having his hectocotylus inserted in the female.

Males demonstrate a clear preference for guarding and mating with large females, which produce more eggs than smaller females. This is true across all octopus species: "Male *Abdopus aculeatus* are known to pull and cannibalize the arms of conspecifics during mate competition."[69] An injury to the hectocotylus can be devastating because it may prevent the male from copulating in the future, which likely explains why males keep the hectocotylus close to their body to protect it while moving about their habitat.

After a successful mating, the female takes shelter in her den and covers the entrance with rocks. She remains in her den for days, spawning thousands of eggs. The female will stay with the eggs until they hatch. She will remain with them, cleaning and caring for them for a short period of time before she dies. Algae octopuses are semelparous, engaging in a single reproductive act before dying.

## BLUEGILLS

The ubiquitous bluegill of North America also has sneaky fucker males. Bluegills are members of the sunfish family and are found in lakes, ponds, rivers, and streams. They are found both in shallow water and deep water, often taking cover among aquatic plants or underwater structures. Bluegills can grow to be a foot long and weigh over four pounds.

*Lepomis macrochirus* is identified by the black spot located at the edge of the gills. The body coloration ranges from purple-blue to dark olive on its sides and face. The breast and abdomen are yellow, but in the case of breeding males, they become bright orange. Bluegills feed on plankton, aquatic insects, and fish. They, in turn, are preyed upon by larger fish, birds, turtles, and humans. I remember catching bluegills at a small lake in Wisconsin with my grandfather. Bluegills possess incredible maneuverability due to the architecture of their fins and body, which allows them to hunt and escape predators.

Breeding season for bluegills begins in late spring and ends in late summer (usually May through August). The males are the first to arrive at the mating site, and they create nests or spawning beds in the gravel or sand in the shallow water. I distinctly remember as a kid watching them make these bowl-shaped depressions in the muddy lake bottom. At the time, I didn't know what they were doing but I was fascinated by the behavior and the aggressiveness with which they protected their underwater nests. Once the males create and establish their nests, they chase anything away that comes close to their territory.

When a female approaches a male's bed, he begins to swim in circles while making grunting sounds. If the female chooses to enter his nest, they will begin to swim around one another. The male is often very aggressive toward the female during this stage of the courtship. If the female decides to stay, they both enter the nest and rest in the middle of the bowl. The pair then engages in copulation, with bellies touching and quivering, and spawning commences. They repeat this process several times, one after another. When the spawning is complete, the male guards the eggs in the nest until the larvae hatch and swim away.

Male bluegills utilize three distinct behavioral patterns when attempting to spawn with females: parental, sneaker, and satellite. Parental males are basically the alphas of the group. They build nests, attract females, and provide parental care to their offspring. These males are often larger, with a bright yellow-orange breast, and they are very aggressive toward other males that come close to their nest territory.

Sneaker males lack the bright breast color and remain close to the substrate. They often hide just outside the rim of the nest, behind plants, rocks, weed beds, and woody debris. From their hiding spots, sneaker males dart out into the nest, attempting to avoid the parental male while releasing sperm. They often swim just beneath the spawning pair. Sneaker males are the smallest and the youngest males, and as they grow older and get larger, they graduate to a new reproductive approach.

Satellite males look like female bluegills and mimic their behavior. With female-like coloration and female-like behavior, these males hope to fool the parental male and gain access to the nest. Satellite males generally hover above the parental male on the nest, waiting for that male to pair up with a female. Then they slowly descend in the water column. The parental male often has trouble discerning between the female and the female-looking satellite male. All three fish circle the nest together while both males release their sperm. If the parental male catches the satellite or sneaker male on the nest, he will aggressively attack the intruder, often inflicting damage.

It is interesting to note that sneakers never become parental males; they graduate to become satellite males. Satellite males also never become parental males, probably because they never reach the body size necessary to create nests, defend nests, and fight off other males. As we have seen in other species, body size impacts reproductive success. Large parental males obtain better, more centralized nests within the colony, which are preferred by females. Female bluegills are quite choosy and generally select males that are larger in size. The size of the female is also important in that larger females can produce 1,000 times more eggs than smaller females.

## RED DEER

The stately red deer (*Cervus elaphus*) is a large deer species native to Europe, Eurasia, and the mountains of Tunisia and Morocco, though it has since been introduced in many other areas around the world. Red deer are herbivores, with a four-chambered stomach and an even number of toes on each hoof. As their name implies, they have reddish-brown coats. The size of red deer varies dramatically depending on the subspecies and region. Males range from six to eight feet in length and can weigh up to 530 pounds. Females are between five and seven feet in length and weigh up to 370 pounds.

Males (stags) have impressive antlers, which they shed every year toward winter's end. Antler growth is associated with testosterone levels and fluctuates as testosterone production increases prior to the rutting season. Males also grow neck manes during the mating season.

Red deer spend the majority of the year separated in male and female groups. During the rut, males and females come together to mate. Stags attempt to gain access to females by roaring and fighting rival males, and serious injuries can occur with the collision of antlers. Prior to engaging in combat, males walk in parallel with one another so they can visually assess the size and strength of their opponent.

Dominant alpha male stags have harems of up to twenty females. Males reach their peak reproductive output at the age of eight. Young males aged four and under and older males aged eleven and above are relegated to the periphery of the harems during the rut.

Being an alpha male takes its toll; harem-holding males rarely have time to eat and therefore lose as much as 20 percent of their body weight during the rut. The stress of their reign at the top can also make them more susceptible to injury and disease. They must enter the breeding season in peak shape to perform optimally and survive.

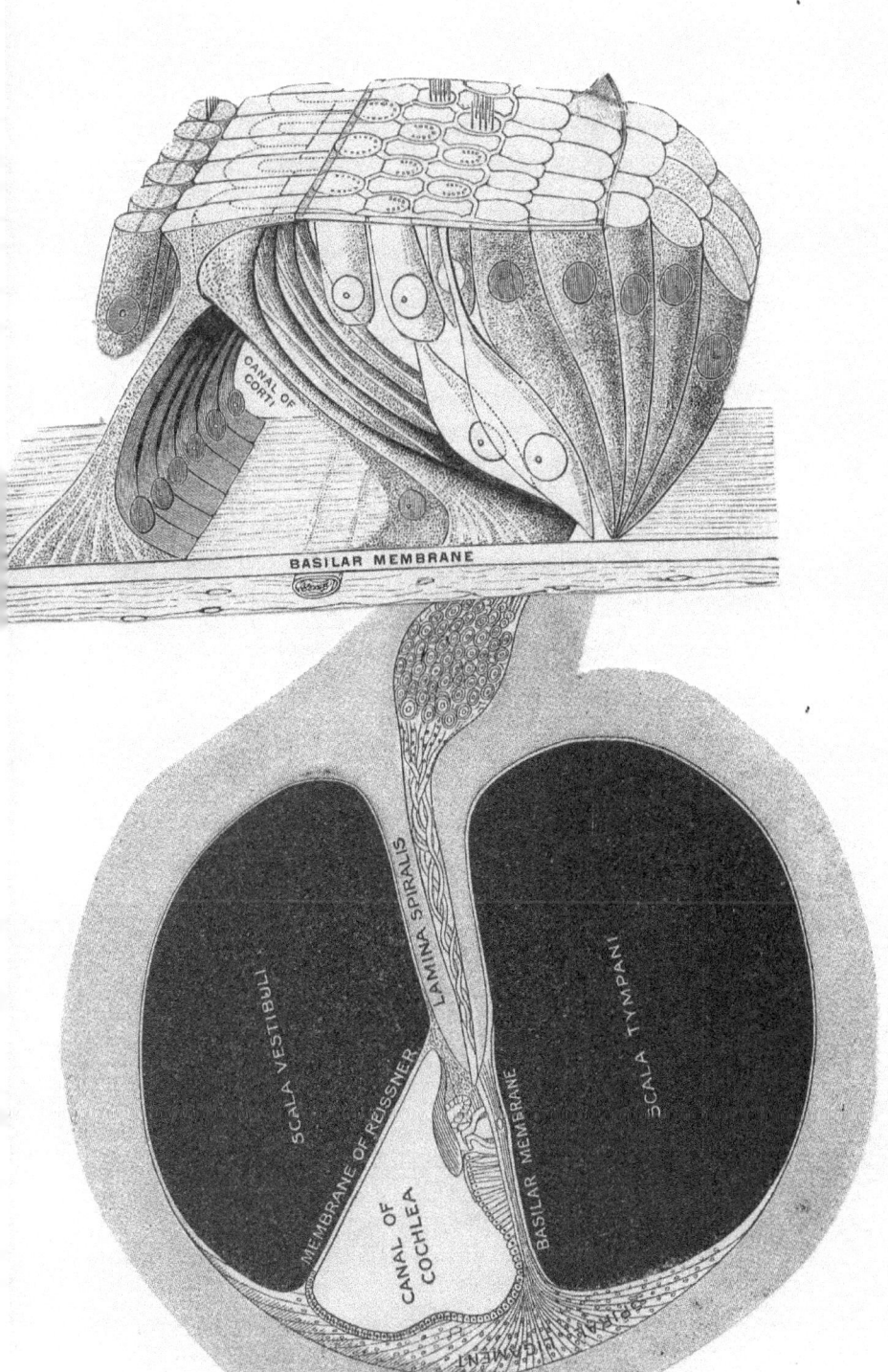

A stag's roar is used to attract females (hinds), to keep his harem together, and to battle other males for position within the dominance hierarchy. Hinds are more attracted to males that roar the loudest and most frequently. The roar of red deer males also serves as an advertisement to competing stags to assess each other's fighting abilities. Roaring contests occur most frequently between two closely matched mature males in prime fighting condition. The stags alternate their roars; the harem-holding male roars, followed by a pause, and then the opponent responds. Roaring contests are often a precursor to fighting. According to biologist Tim Clutton-Brock, "Most harem-holders have to defend their harems once every 4–6 days."[70]

Scientists have identified four categories of male red deer: primary stags, secondary stags, tertiary stags, and opportunist stags (also known as sneaky fuckers). The primary red deer stags are the alphas. They are larger and more powerful; they roar the loudest and are the first to establish harems. Secondary stags are also quite large and typically are the ones to challenge the alphas. A secondary stag typically defeats the primary male when he becomes exhausted from fighting off rival males and tending to the harem. A tertiary male takes control of the harem when the secondary stag declines.

Opportunistic males only come into contact with hinds by chance. We can follow bloodlines with incredible accuracy using genetic fingerprinting technology, making it possible to pinpoint precisely which stag in a herd was the father of a certain fawn, so we know that other, weaker males are having sexual relations with females while the dominant male is off battling other males, staking out territory, and yelling masterful calls through the forest. This is referred to as the Sneaky Fucker Theory, with all the calm, careful categorization for which the scientific community is famed.

## HUMAN SNEAKY FUCKERS

The sneaky fucker theory applies to humans as well. As we have seen in red deer, octopus, and bluegills, males find novel ways to gain sexual access to females. Human males are no different. Ancestral males spent a lot of time away from females, hunting for food or fighting battles. The males that did not hunt and fight stayed behind with the women and children and kept them company, socializing with the females, providing comfort and showing an interest in their personal lives. These men were considered to be more effeminate, however, many of these same men also had reproductive and sexual success—in some cases, an even higher rate of success than the more "masculine" men. Preeminent biologist Richard Dawkins theorizes that the "gay gene" was passed down through the generations when the dominant males were off hunting while the "trusted" gay males were left with females. Some of the gay men then reproduced with women, and the "gay gene" was passed down to the next generation. For some people, sexual orientation and attraction are very fixed, but other people's sexual orientation and desires might be fluid and change over time.

Canadian professor Gad Saad used the behavior of male social justice warriors as an example of the sneaky fucker theory at work. These social justice warrior males memorize all the appropriate responses to use when attempting to win a woman's trust. They take satisfaction in calling out male privilege and problematic behavior by the patriarchy and posing as sensitive, socially conscious "allies." Any indication of their masculinity will be hidden. There are countless examples of less dominant, lower-ranking males in the social hierarchy that take advantage of opportunities to mate with females while dominant males are off occupied with other things.

Sneaker males in many ways have become ubiquitous in modern society and have permeated many social arenas: they are students, politicians, entrepreneurs, entertainers, sport figures, religious people, and traders. Cheating your way to the top has become an accepted life strategy. Anonymous individual critics undermine the respect for simple, honest work. In the wild, the young are kept in check through the hierarchy and the elders. In modern times, very few young adults learn to farm, hunt, fish, apprentice into jobs, get drafted into the military, or perform manual labor. Historically, these types of jobs were often done under the mentorship of experienced adults. Nowadays the youth have so much freedom and control and yet are riddled with insecurity, confusion, and depression.

## CONCLUSION

What might be the benefits for sneaker males among humans? If a male is smaller in stature and weaker, he benefits from this opportunistic approach. Sneaker males may even do better than average, conventional males in terms of reproductive success. A female's kind, effeminate male friend may be able to sneak a copulation while the dominant male is away.

Biologist and author Delia Owens sums it up like this: "However, some stunted males, not strong, adorned, or smart enough to hold good territories, possess bags of tricks to fool the females. They parade their smaller forms around in pumped-up postures or shout frequently—even if in shrill voices. By relying on pretense and false signals, they manage to grab a copulation here or there."[71] The same applies to humans. There are some males that live at home with their parents but run out and rent a Lamborghini for a night to pull up at the clubs in hopes of deceiving females with this display of wealth. It often works for these sneaky fuckers. Other males adorn themselves with fancy clothes and jewelry, again, in hopes of attracting a choosy female. These displays, even if fake, have some level of success. Low-status males of many species, including ours, attempt to use deception as a way to land a mate.

# PART IV
# GENDER MATTERS

# TEN
# POLYGYNY

*"Being powerful is like being a lady. If you have to tell people you are, you aren't."*

—MARGARET THATCHER

## POLYGYNY

Before we define *polygyny*, let's take a step back and look at some other words that are often confused with it. *Polygamy* is when a person has more than one spouse of either gender. *Polyandry* is when a woman has more than one husband, and polygyny is when a man has more than one wife. Polyandry is not as common as polygyny, but both are still found in human populations around the world. Polyandry is currently practiced in Nepal, China, Nigeria, Cameroon, India, Kenya and Tanzania. It is not uncommon for a woman to be married to two or more men who are brothers, which is termed fraternal polyandry.

When discussing human mating systems, *Homo sapiens* are considered to be a primarily monogamous species. That being said, humans are also moderately polygynous. Polygyny is widespread in Africa, found in countries such as Kenya, Nigeria, Malawi, South Africa, Somalia, and Mozambique. Many majority Muslim countries allow polygyny with up to four wives. Polygyny is also found in India, Russia, and China (although it is illegal, it's not enforced). It is practiced in Bosnia and Herzegovina among Muslims and in Chile by the Mapuche people. In the United States, some Mormons are polygynous (although this practice is illegal and no longer endorsed by the Mormon church).

Men who practice polygyny are generally older than men who practice monogamy because it takes time to acquire the sufficient resources to attract wives. Ancestral women preferred men with resources because it aided with their survival and reproduction. The burden of reproduction falls most heavily on the female: internal fertilization, nine-month gestation, and lactation. Hierarchies are universal features of human groups. More resources go to those that are high in the hierarchy, so social status and resource potential are forever linked.

In humans, mating strategies change depending on the ratio of the sexes. In most polygynous societies, the most sought-after women marry right after puberty, which can create a situation where single men have a hard time finding a desirable mate. Mate shortages, male or female, often dictate the type of mating strategy that is employed. If men outnumber women, monogamy is more common. If women outnumber men, men may be reluctant to commit to one woman and pursue many casual relationships.

Men who are in polygynous marriages are at risk of being cuckolded and, in turn, humiliated. The greater the number of wives that a man has, the greater the probability that one of his wives will seek out an extra-pair copulation. As evolutionary psychologist David Buss states, "In a polygynous marriage, for example, killing an unfaithful wife might salvage a man's honor and also serve as a powerful deterrent to infidelity by his other wives. Polygynous men who took no action may have risked being cuckolded with impunity in the future. In some circumstances in our evolutionary past, killing a wife may have represented an effort at damage containment designed to stop the hemorrhaging of reproductive resources."[72]

Polygyny has been identified as a major sociocultural predictor of violence towards intimate partners. A study by researcher Bright Opoku Ahinkorah in sub-Saharan Africa discovered a strong link between polygyny and aggression against intimate partners, and the United Nations Office on Drugs and Crime reports 47,000 women and girls were murdered by their intimate partners or other family members in 2020 globally.[73]

Polygyny is still a common practice in many places around the world. One study of over 800 cultures found that more than 80 percent of them engaged in polygynous relationships. Even

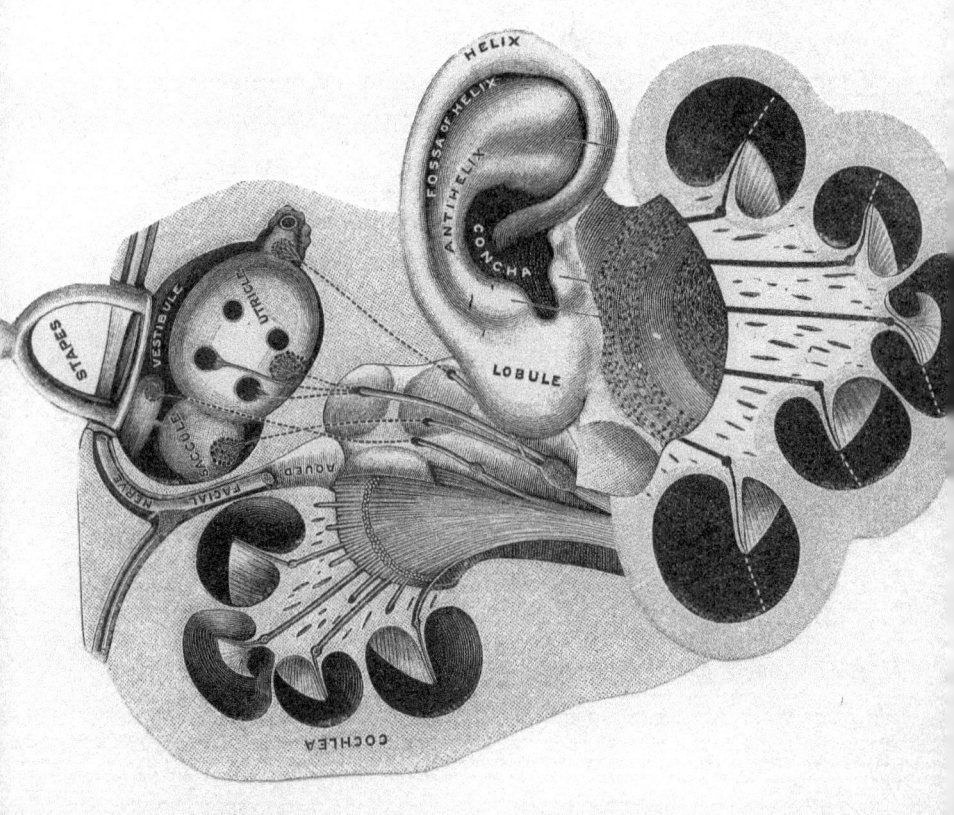

in countries where it is prohibited, it still occurs and is tolerated without punishment.

From a female's perspective, polygyny can be either beneficial or detrimental. It is detrimental if her husband's additional wives take away resources that could be going to her and her children but beneficial in cultures where polygynous men allocate their resources equally across all of their wives.

Polygynous societies where a male is married to multiple females up the ante on male competition and the risky tactics that are associated with it. The risks that males take competing with other males over access to females contributes to the mortality differences found between the sexes. The sex differences are magnified in highly polygynous cultures. Scientists Joseph Plavcan and Carel van Schaik found that in situations where there is greater male-to-male competition, hazardous male behavior, and larger size, there are also higher male mortality rates compared to females—and this is all connected with higher levels of polygyny in a species.[74] A study conducted by Jacob Moorad and other scientists found that polygyny among Mormons in the 1800s benefited male fitness strongly, whereas female fitness was slightly negatively impacted.[75]

## ELEPHANT SEALS

You may not be surprised to find that humans are not the only species practicing polygyny. Elephant seals (*Mirounga angustirostris*) earned their name because of the large noses adorned by males that resemble an elephant's trunk. The elephant seal's proboscis (his enormous nose) begins to grow at sexual maturity (between three and five years old) and is fully grown by seven to nine years old. The male nose is actually a secondary sexual characteristic: males with the largest proboscis are often able to intimidate other males simply by merit of the size of their nose and thereby avoid unwanted or unnecessary confrontations.

Elephant seals are one of the most sexually dimorphic species on the planet, with a tremendous size discrepancy between the sexes: males are generally three times larger than females. A male elephant seal can weigh up to 5,000 pounds, reaching an astonishing length of sixteen feet. By comparison, females tend to weigh near 1,800 pounds and reach the relatively modest length of twelve feet.

The northern elephant seal is the second largest seal in the world and ranges over the Pacific coast of North America. Elephant seals are notable for their round faces and extremely large eyes. Apart from making them quite striking and affable in appearance, there is also an elegant purpose to those big, round eyes: they contain a large number of rods, which aid their perception when they swim beneath the darkened depths of the ocean.

Pups are born with a black coat, which turns silvery brown within a year. Once the pups are weaned, they gather together in weaner pods for safety. The life of a young elephant seal can be fraught with hazard and violence. Generally, one in ten pups will be lost to the pressures of predation, isolation, or even the topography of the beaches themselves. Aggressive males can accidentally crush unwary pups.

Elephant seals spend a remarkable amount of time out in the open sea—up to 80 percent of their life in the vast ocean depths. They often dive to extraordinary depths in search of food and take full advantage of several adaptations that allow them to routinely reach depths of 2,000 feet and remain completely submerged for an astounding 120 minutes. Elephant seals carry the essential oxygen they need within their blood, not in their lungs, and when necessary, they can reduce their heart rate to an incredible four to fifteen beats per minute. Compare that to a healthy human's resting heart rate of around sixty beats per minute.

Throughout the year, elephant seals complete two trips between their feeding grounds and land: during breeding and molting seasons. Females journey over 11,000 miles, while the more massive (and hungrier) males travel 13,000 miles. Adult males return to the breeding grounds in late November, and pregnant females come ashore in late December through early February. Males will spend the next three months battling for supremacy.

Only mature bulls aged eight to nine can compete for alpha status. Males use physical posturing such as rearing up on their hind quarters, vocalizations with bellowing threats, and fights to determine their place in the hierarchy. When fights do occur, they are often violent, bloody contests. Males rear their necks, slashing at one another's chest shields with their large canine teeth. Battles can last from a few minutes up to an hour and continue until one bull is either forced into the water or herded away submissively.

Dominant alpha bulls maintain extensive harems of twenty-five to fifty females. Opportunistic beta males usually lurk around the perimeter of the beach-master's harem and are generally tolerated by stronger alpha males because they, in turn, help discourage the attention of even lower-ranking males. These hopeful beta males cunningly aspire to get access to females when the alpha male is otherwise occupied with fighting or mating. Still, their chances are bleak indeed, as nine out of ten males never even get the chance to mate. Bachelor pods consist of males that are either too old or too young to challenge the alpha males for access to females.

Courtship in elephant seals is unsubtle, direct, and often harsh. A male approaches the side of a female and then puts a foreflipper on her back, bites her neck, and pulls her close. He then attempts to copulate with the female. Impregnated females return to the beach eleven months later to birth their pups.

Although once abundant, in 1910, there were fewer than 1,000 elephant seals on the Pacific Coast. They were almost hunted to extinction for their blubber. Over 200 gallons of high-quality oil could be obtained from one male elephant seal. Today, their population has grown to an estimated 150,000 individuals because of protections put in place in the 1920s and 1970s by the governments of Mexico and the United States.

## LIONS

The male lion is an iconic image. It is used on everything from avatars to flags to logos to movies to paintings to beers. The so-called King of the Jungle, the lion is associated with strength, power, fear, and masculinity and is both revered and feared. It is one of the few predators that kills humans. Hearing a lion roar triggers something in humans' primal lizard brain. It makes the hair stand up on the back of your neck. Lions are impressive animals, and most human males relish the idea of being compared to a lion, even if undeservedly so.

Lions (*Panthera leo*) were once found across the entire continent of Africa except in the desert and equatorial rainforests. They also were found in the Middle East and in a large swath from India all the way to Greece. The mighty cat is now only found in a smattering of places in Africa.

Lions are primarily found in savanna ecosystems but also inhabit mountains, forests, and semi-deserts. They are muscular, powerful, large cats with tan fur and white underbellies. They have long tails tipped with black tufts of fur. Male lions grow manes around the age of three, which is associated with testosterone production and varies depending on geographic region.

Lions are a sexually dimorphic species. Males range in weight from 150–260 kilograms, and females weigh 122–182 kilograms. The head and body length of males is 1.72–2.50 meters, while in females it is 1.58–1.92 meters. Lions fuel these large bodies with meat, as they are predatory carnivores. Female lions do most of the hunting, both in groups and as individuals. Lions feed on many different types of prey, including wildebeests, zebras, impalas, cape buffalo, rodents, fish, eggs, and birds. They also scavenge for food.

Lions are social, gregarious, matriarchal mammals. Most lions live in prides, which are groups of lions usually consisting of one or two males, four or five females, and some juveniles and cubs.

Males form coalitions with other males to take over a pride. The first order of business for the males taking over a pride is to kill all the cubs, which causes the females to enter estrus soon after this event. The new male then impregnates the females with his future progeny. A male's reign at the top is brief, with most only lasting two years.

Lion vocalizations express a wide range of emotions—very similar to humans—depending on the intonation, volume, and speed of the call. They utilize many forms of vocalization, from roaring to purring to woofing to growling to grunting. A lion's roar is one of the most recognizable sounds in all of nature and is used to advertise territories, communicate location to other pride members, scare off rivals, and strengthen social bonds. Lions roar most frequently at night, when they are most active, or right before dawn. Both males and females roar, but the male's roar is deeper and louder and can carry up to eight kilometers. Females grunt to call for their cubs and communicate to close-by adults. Purring, like house cats, is a sound of contentment.

Lions also use chemical communication in the form of urine scent marking and raking trees and the ground. Males primarily scent mark bushes and trees during their patrols defending their territory. A male lion's strut is another dominance display, during which he takes a tall posture, walking erect around the female with his tail held high. A male's physical size and robust mane also signify dominance.

Lions copulate frequently; scientists estimate that there are 3,000 copulations for one cub to survive to the ripe old age of one year. Mortality is very high among cubs, which face threats from other lions, predation, and starvation. Up to 80 percent of cubs die before reaching their second birthday. When a female in the pride enters estrus, which usually lasts around four days, the first male member of the pride to reach her gains mating priority. Often there is only one dominant male in the pride with some juvenile males, so the alpha male has first and only access to the females in heat.

The large, showy male lion is an iconic image etched into the minds of humans throughout the world. Their sheer size and mane make them less effective hunters than the females, but they evolved this way for a different reason. They are the product of sexual selection. Male lions look the way that they do simply for the opportunity to rule over a pride and thereby have mating access to many females.

## HORSES

The horse (*Equus caballus*) is also an iconic animal. Horses have changed the course of human history. They have been an essential part of human migration, sports, work (a true beast of burden), warfare (unquestionably a game changer on the battlefield), entertainment (in the form of television, film, and literature), psychotherapy, and products such as food, leather, and glue. The economic impact of horses is staggering. The American Horse Council estimates that horses directly impact the economy of the United States to the tune of $39 billion and indirectly impact it by over $102 billion.[76]

Horses are beloved by humans across the globe. Riding a horse in nature is an exhilarating experience. You feel closer to nature. The disconnect of being in a vehicle is gone. I have been fortunate to have ridden horses in many countries around the world. I'll never forget riding in Ethiopia. I was watching black-and-white colobus monkeys in the trees when we rode out into a clearing and were suddenly passed by a massive group of baboons making their way through the grasses. It was a surreal feeling to be surrounded by a troop of baboons while on horseback.

The horse's strength, speed, endurance, and carrying capacity have made a major contribution to human civilization. Horses are so strong that we use the word *horsepower* to refer to the amount of power that an engine produces. The term *horsepower* was first used in the 1700s by Scottish inventor James Watt. Watt settled on how much weight a horse can lift while pulling a rope through a pulley attached to a weight on the ground. One mechanical horsepower lifts 550 pounds by one foot in one second.

Humans originally just looked at horses as a source of food. Early humans, who were hunter-gatherers, hunted horses and other herbivores for meat while they tried to avoid being eaten by predators. On horseback, humans became better hunters and more deadly warriors. In many cultures, horses became a symbol of status, with ownership and riding privileges reserved for nobility and warriors. Warfare was forever changed with cavalries and war chariots.

Not only did horses change warfare, but they also changed agriculture by plowing fields, long-distance transportation via stagecoaches, and communication through the Pony Express.

Horses originated on what is now known as the continent of North America some 35–55 million years ago. They were once the size of dogs adapted for forest life. Over millions of years, they increased in size, diversified, and spread to other regions of the world. Horses primarily feed on grasses and have adapted to a wide variety of habitats including grasslands, savannas, swamps, woodlands, and semi-deserts.

A horse's physical shape is unmistakable: a muscular body with short hair, four long and slender legs, and a long tail. The other notable features are their hooves and manes. Since their domestication, horses come in a wide variety of colors and sizes. Coat color ranges from white to brown, red, and black and can be spotted and patterned. Horses vary dramatically in size as well; they can be anywhere from 230–900 kilograms (500–2,000 pounds) and 220–280 centimeters (85–110 inches) tall. Horses typically have a lifespan of twenty-five to thirty years.

Much like lions and humans, horses are also social animals. They form herds (known as bands) and create social hierarchies. A typical band consists of one to four stallions and five to eleven mares and juveniles. An alpha male is dominant over the herd, followed by other males, reproductive females, non-reproductive females, and juveniles.

As with other species, alpha males expend significantly more energy than other members of the hierarchy. In horses, alpha males are on the move up to 45 percent of the time, versus other members of the herd that move around less than 10 percent of the time.

Alpha males are also deprived of sleep; they spend only 5–6 percent of their time sleeping, compared to other members of the band which sleep 20–27 percent of the time. Alpha males also burn up a tremendous amount of energy rounding up females and defending them from rival males during the breeding season. Alpha males generally travel at the back of the band except when a potential threat presents itself. During these moments, the alpha male moves to the front of the band to signal to the rest of the band to flee. In some cases he even attacks the threat to protect the band.

Horses communicate primarily through vocalizations and head movements. During the breeding season, male horses increase their vocalizations via grunts and screams and also utter their characteristic neigh or whinny in the presence of females who are in estrus. They also become more physically aggressive, stomping and pawing at the ground.

Females may scream and kick at the unwanted advances of a male during breeding season. Band members jockey to establish or reinforce the hierarchy and assert dominance. One clear sign of dominance occurs when a dominant horse lays its head on the back end of the lower-ranking individual.

Since horses are prey animals, they have very keen senses. Horses have extremely large eyes—the largest of any land mammal. The positioning of their eyes allows them to have a range of vision, both binocular and monocular. This means they can see well at night and during the day.

Their vision is the primary means of perceiving the environment. A horse's hearing is also quite good. Their ears are long and slender and capable of rotating in different directions to pick up sounds. Their sense of smell is not as robust as their vision or hearing but plays an important role in picking up scents in the environment and in social interactions with other horses.

Horses exhibit a polygynous mating system, similar to what we have seen with lions and elephant seals. Males herd the females during the breeding season and defend them from rival males. Males avoid herding related horses to avoid inbreeding. As with many male mammals, they fight with other males over access to reproductive females. Alpha males violently kick and bite other males as they fight over herds—specifically the females within those herds.

As we have seen with countless examples in this book, hierarchy influences reproductive status and reproductive success. Alpha males control access to the best resources, so females and their foals get priority access to resources.

## CONCLUSION

As we have seen, polygyny exists across many species, including humans. One of the strongest and quickest evolutionary processes is sexual selection, or competition between individuals of one sex for reproductive access to individuals of the other. In humans, a risky tactic might sometimes be the only method to acquire the social standing or resources necessary to find a mate to give birth to viable offspring. For example, we know that greater levels of polygyny in a species leads to an increase in male–male competition, risky male behavior, larger-sized male individuals, and greater male mortality when compared to females. Male lions, horses, and elephant seals are all very large, and the males all compete quite vigorously against one another for access to females. There are many parallels between the polygynous males of elephant seals, lions, and horses and the human males that practice polygyny. Polygynous human males also compete with one another, are larger than females, and experience greater mortality than females.

The human mating system is complex and beautiful in some ways but straightforward and ugly in others. There will always be conflict between males and females. Within the sexes there is also competition and conflict—males competing with males and females competing with females. The reality is that desirable males and females will always be in demand but there will not be enough of them to meet the needs of the others. Stunningly beautiful women attract the attention of many men but only a few men will be successful in attracting those women.

# ELEVEN
# ALPHA INVERSIONS

> "At the violet hour, when the eyes and back
> Turn upward from the desk,
> when the human engine waits
> Like a taxi throbbing waiting,
> I Tiresias, though blind, throbbing between
> two lives."
> —T. S. ELIOT

## TIRESIAS

Tiresias was a famous prophet in Greek mythology. One day, Tiresias was out for a hike when off of the side of the path he noticed two snakes copulating. For some reason, Tiresias took exception to this and hit the snakes with his walking staff. This angered the goddess Hera, so she transformed him into a woman. As a woman, Tiresias got married and had children. After seven years, she was out walking and again came across some mating snakes, but this time she left them alone, and she was transformed back into a man.

Having lived as both a man and as a woman provided the experience that would ultimately lead to Tiresias's blindness. Hera was arguing with Zeus over who enjoyed sex more, males or females, and called upon Tiresias to settle the argument once and for all. Hera believed that men enjoyed sex more than women, while Zeus thought that women enjoyed sex more than men. Tiresias was in a unique position to settle this dispute, having experienced sex both as a man and as a woman.

Unfortunately for Tiresias, his answer did not please Hera. He said that women derive more pleasure out of sex than men, siding with Zeus. This so angered Hera that she struck Tiresias blind. Zeus felt sorry for Tiresias, but there was little he could do because one god cannot cancel out what another god has done. Since Zeus could not undo the blindness, he decided that he could give Tiresias something else: he gave him the ability to see the future. Zeus also gave him the gifts of prophecy and longevity. Tiresias lived for 175 years as a blind prophet in Thebes, a city in central Greece.

I think the myth of Tiresias teaches some important lessons. The first lesson is never to cause harm to animals or nature. The second lesson is that it could be a good idea to at least try for a little while to see things from the perspective of the other sex. The

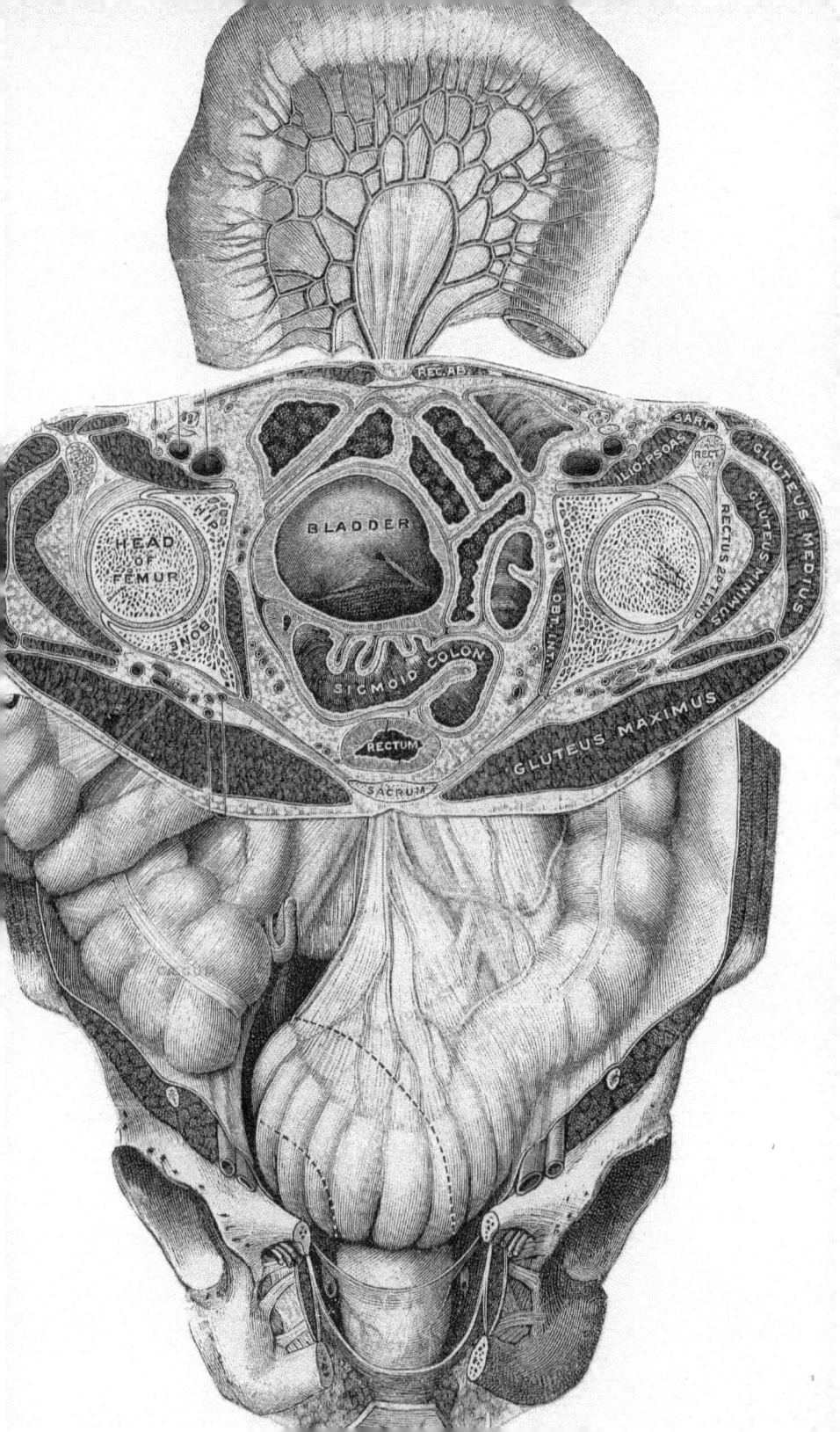

final lesson is that if given a second chance, as Tiresias was, when he saw the snakes again, he did not bother them.

Having learned his lesson, Tiresias was granted back his masculinity by the gods. As we will see below, nature manifests itself in many unique and interesting ways with many lessons to be learned.

## BLUE-HEADED WRASSE

Around 500 species of fish are capable of changing sex. The most common change in gender goes from female fish turning into males, but there are some species where that is the reverse. In blue-headed wrasse (*Thalassoma bifasciatum*), females turn into males under specific conditions.

Blue-headed wrasses have a complex mating system and are notable in that they are a protogynous sequential hermaphrodite. So let's break this down: the genus *Thalassoma* comes from the Greek words *thalassa*, which means "the sea" and *soma* which means "body." The species name *bifasciatum* comes from the Latin word *bifasciatus*, which means "formed of two bundles." Protogynous means that female reproductive organs mature before the male reproductive organs. A hermaphrodite is an organism that has both male and female sex organs. When put together, protogynous hermaphrodites are animals (in this case, the wrasse fish) that are born as females and at some point in their lifespan change sex to males.

The blue-headed wrasse is a common schooling reef fish found in the coral reefs of the Caribbean and the Gulf of Mexico. They have a variety of color patterns based on their life phase and behavior.

Blue-headed wrasse adults have blue heads and green bodies, separated by two dark vertical stripes with a white bar in the middle. Only a small percentage (4 percent) of fish actually reach this stage, often called the supermale or terminal-phase male. Juvenile blue-headed wrasses are yellow with a black spot on their dorsal fin. Small males and females have a horizontal stripe that is broken up into blotches, with a variation of white and yellow head and body.

Blue-headed wrasses experience three life stages: the juvenile phase, the initial phase, and the terminal phase. Individuals can reach sexual maturity at a length as small as 1.5 inches. Blue-headed wrasses spawn throughout the year. Once again, blue-headed wrasses use different mating strategies depending on the size and dominance of the male. At midday, large numbers of females and small males jut toward the surface of the water, releasing sperm and eggs. Larger males spawn in pairs of a single male and a single female. The dominant or supermale forms a harem and spawns with one female at a time. A male courts a female by performing a dashing behavior; if she is receptive, she joins the male in a dash toward the surface to release her eggs while he releases his sperm. Supermales spawn with thirty to fifty females in a single day but can spawn with up to 100. The fertilized eggs float in the water column for a period of six to eight weeks, and then the fry burrow into the sand for protection and transition to the juvenile stage. The juveniles then congregate among the seagrass and coral reefs as they continue their maturation process.

Within the social hierarchy of males, terminal-phase males are the most aggressive and have the highest ranking: the alpha. Large terminal-phase males defend territories and form harems for mating. The lower-ranking initial-phase males employ a different tactic for mating, using spawning rushes in larger groups. Blue-headed wrasses are capable of reproducing in four different ways throughout their lifetime: as a female in a group spawning event, as a female in a pair spawning event within the territory of a large male, as a small male in a group spawning event, and lastly as a dominant terminal male in a pair spawning event within his territory. Once again, nature finds a way. Small males release more sperm than large terminal males to compete with all the other small males at the spawning events. An alpha blue-head wrasse only competes with other males prior to spawning and only spawns with the female when there are no other males around, so he does not have to produce as much sperm.

What causes the sex change in blue-headed wrasses? Scientists figured out when they removed terminal (alpha) males from a population, it triggered females to change sex. They discovered that when the males are removed, females become stressed and in turn become more aggressive and start to perform male courtship behaviors. The female individuals that display these behaviors become dominant in the social hierarchy, and after a couple of days, the genes that are associated with female hormones shut down and their colors begin to change from yellow and brown to the typical male coloration of green and blue.

As the changes in behavior and coloration are occurring in conjunction with the cessation of female hormone production, the egg-producing tissues in their ovaries start to shrink and are replaced by sperm-producing tissues. In as little as eight days, the mature ovaries of the female are transformed into testes. This newly minted male can now mate with females and sire offspring. It takes around twenty days for the complete process to take place; the full male coloration takes longer than the ovary-to-testes transformation. This speedy metamorphosis is unique to bluehead wrasses—other species take much longer.

## FLATWORMS

Another organism with an interesting mating system is the flatworm from the phylum *Platyhelminthes*. Flatworms are a diverse group of animals that are aquatic and terrestrial in moist environments. Terrestrial flatworms need moisture to survive, so they are most likely to be found under rocks in leaf litter where the environment generally remains damp or wet. True to their name, flatworms are limbless animals with a flattened appearance. As with most worms, their bodies are covered in a slime-like substance that helps with locomotion and keeps them from drying out. Flatworms vary widely in size and shape; they can range from a few millimeters to over a foot long. Some resemble a leaf with a wide middle and pointed ends, while others are thin and long, and some have a hammerhead. Flatworm coloration is also diverse, with some being gray, brown, blue, black, orange, yellow, or striped. Depending on the species, some flatworms have a pair of eyes, and some have numerous small eyes concentrated around the head.

Flatworms are bilaterally symmetrical organisms. This means that their left side and right side are mirror images of one another. They have a dorsal and ventral side as well as a head and tail end. They have no body cavity and lack a respiratory and circulatory system; these functions take place by absorption through the body wall. The mouth is curiously located in the middle of the underside of their body. This single digestive cavity is responsible for both ingestion and egestion. Yes, that is what you are thinking, most flatworms do not have an anus so undigested wastes are expelled through the mouth. Free-living flatworms wrap around their prey, such as earthworms, snails, and slugs, and digest it by sucking up the liquified contents with their tube-like mouth.

Flatworms include some species that are nonparasitic, free-living animals and others that are entirely parasitic. They are hermaphrodites and possess both male and female reproductive organs. Most flatworms can reproduce sexually or asexually. Asexual reproduction is the more common of the two forms, occurring when the body divides and each part becomes a new worm. Sexual reproduction occurs when they mate and lay cocoons containing numerous offspring.

Some aquatic flatworm species mate via penis fencing, which is similar to a sword fight, in which a duel takes place, with each participant trying to impregnate the other. The loser of this contest adopts the female role of developing the eggs.

The marine flatworm (*Pseudoceros bifurcus*) has two penises that look like white spikes located on the underside of its head. Just before engaging in a duel, the two flatworms rear up and evert their penises, attempting to inseminate their opponent while avoiding being inseminated. These penis-fencing contests can last for hours. It is a stab-or-be-stabbed type of sexual interaction, and sperm transfer occurs once the penis is inserted into the body of the combatant.

Now, you are probably wondering if they ever both stab each other, and the answer is yes. On the occasions where they both stab each other, there is a distinct benefit to being the first to strike. Researchers have discovered that the first to inseminate acquires a longer injection time than the second, even though reciprocal penis insertion could be accomplished by the second partner. Scientists Nico Michiels and Leslie Newman stated, "The asymmetrical outcome of inseminations favors animals that inject first, as they will father more eggs in more partners and have fewer wounds to heal." They go on to say, "Hypodermic insemination, when present, allows hermaphrodites to skew sexual interactions in favor of sperm donation, fuelling an evolutionary arms race between strike and avoidance behavior."[77] Penis fencing is an effort to boost the advantages of sperm donation above the expense of sperm procurement. While the father has no obligation, the flatworm that receives the sperm must pay for the costs of wound healing from all of the jabbing and loses control over fertilization. As a result, he must raise the young and take care of the developing eggs.

A study conducted by Nico Michiels and Blanka Bakovski on sperm trading in *Schmidtea polychroa* suggests that the digestion of sperm may boost sperm production.[78] Flatworms that received sperm from previous matings had more of their own sperm to distribute in future matings.

## GARDEN SNAILS

As we have seen throughout this book, the natural world is replete with examples of extraordinary and sometimes strange mating behaviors. The common garden snail (*Cornu aspersum*) has a piercing way of love. The garden snail was at one time classified under *Helix aspersa*, but is now classified as *Cornu aspersum*. It is one of the best-known and most prolific terrestrial mollusks on the planet.

The garden snail is native to Europe but is now found throughout the world. This species has a hard but thin shell, approximately 1 inch in diameter by 1.5 inches high with the classic spherical, whorl shape. The shell varies in color from dark brown to light brown or often golden with brown and yellow stripes. The soft body of the garden snail is brownish and covered in a slimy mucus.

They move with a gliding motion powered by their muscular "foot" and aided by their mucus, which reduces their friction as they move around, leaving behind the infamous snail trail. Mucus is constantly secreted by glands in the foot.

The garden snail, as the name implies, is a plant feeder, consuming everything from herbs to fruit trees, flowers, tree bark, and occasionally decomposing organic matter. During times of activity such as moving or feeding, the foot and the head emerge from the shell. The head has four tentacles: two are used for sensing light, and the other two are used for touch and smell.

The garden snail's mouth resides beneath its tentacles and has something called a radula, which is similar to a tongue but is more like a hardened, toothed ribbon with which it scrapes and fragments its food. When threatened or when experiencing extreme weather conditions, the snail retracts into its shell. During drought periods or when the temperatures drop below freezing, the garden snail can survive by entering a state of inactivity, similar to hibernation. Most garden snails also enter a period of dormancy during the winter months, known as overwintering.

Garden snails, much like other gastropod mollusks, are hermaphrodites. Since they have both male and female reproductive organs, they can produce the reproductive gametes of both sexes. Although they are capable of self-fertilization, they usually mate with another snail for fertilization.

Garden snails begin their reproductive journey between their first and second year of life, when they reach sexual maturity. The breeding season takes place at the beginning of the summer. During the courtship phase, two snails will touch each other and then insert something called a love dart into their partner. The mating ritual is actually quite involved, occurring over six hours, beginning with circling one another followed by the touching of tentacles and the biting of lips.

As the snails are performing their mating dance, they are trying to maneuver their genital pore, located below the head, into a position where it will be touched by their partner, which in turn triggers the firing of the love dart, a mucus-covered calcium structure resembling a sword. Love darts are kept within an internal dart sac. Garden snails do not have good aim and therefore often miss the target entirely or fail to penetrate the skin. After firing their love darts, garden snails will often have to mate without firing another dart since it takes a week for another dart to be produced.

Once both snails have fired their darts, they begin copulating. They both insert their penis into their partner and transfer sperm. From start to finish, the mating process can take up to twelve hours. At this point they have both fertilized one another's eggs. Six days after fertilization, oviposition occurs, with each snail depositing around eighty eggs into nests that they dig out with their foot. The eggs hatch after about two weeks.

What is the purpose of snails shooting love darts into their partners? This question has perplexed scientists for years. It is speculated that early Greek scientists were the first to observe the love dart in the garden snail, as it is native to this region. These observations by the Greeks may have been the impetus for the myth of Cupid.

## CUPID

In Greek mythology, Cupid is known as Eros. His origin is murky; depending on the source, he is either the product of asexual reproduction via an egg, or he is the son of Aphrodite and Ares. In Roman mythology, he is the god of love in all of its variations.

Cupid is said to have had a quiver full of arrows; however, there were two different sets of arrows within this array. One set of arrows was golden, and those who were struck with this type of arrow would arouse desire and fall in love, while those struck with the leaden arrow would ignite aversion and fall out of love. It was said that his arrows worked on both mortals and gods.

One story from ancient Greek mythology illustrates this point. The god Apollo was bragging to Eros about how big and strong he was in battle, so Eros decided to teach him a lesson in humility. Eros shot a golden arrow at Apollo, who then fell madly in love with Daphne, a nymph who was associated with bodies of fresh water and was the daughter of the river god Peneus. This would seem relatively harmless, but then Eros struck Daphne with a leaden arrow, which caused her to be repulsed by Apollo. Daphne grew tired of Apollo's infatuation and continued pursuit, so she pleaded with her father for help. Peneus finally obliged, transforming her into a laurel tree. Although Apollo was heartbroken that his love was a tree, he still loved the tree and decided to honor himself and other victors with a wreath of laurel to be worn on the head. The bay laurel (*Laurus nobilis*) is common throughout the Mediterranean as food, for ornamental purposes, and medicinal uses as well.

Garden snail love darts were thought to serve a similar purpose to the love arrows of Eros, creating a passion and sexual awakening in the recipient. The work of Ronald Chase has revealed that the mucus that coats the dart is significant. "The mucus carries an allohormone that is transferred into the recipient's hemolymph when the dart is inserted, which reconfigures the recipient's reproductive system: the bursa copulax (sperm digestion organ) becomes closed off, and the copulatory canal (leading to the sperm storage) is opened."[79] What this means is that more sperm are able to fertilize eggs versus being digested, thereby increasing their paternity. The love dart (gypsobelum) is used to increase the reproductive success of the shooter. Garden snails that misfire their love darts are at a distinct disadvantage. Studies have shown that successful shooters have higher paternity scores. Further studies need to be conducted to see if cryptic female choice plays a role in garden snail reproduction. Theoretically it would make sense that females with internal fertilization would choose "good" sperm to fertilize their eggs to increase their reproductive success.

## CONCLUSION

There are an endless number of ways in which organisms can reproduce and even change sex. We learned that in the blue-headed wrasse, a female can become a male when the dominant male is removed. The female's behavior is the first thing to change, as she becomes more aggressive and starts to perform male courtship behaviors, and very quickly her ovaries transform into testes. We learned of the peculiar practice of penis fencing in flatworms and the odd foreplay of firing love darts in garden snails.

Mythological stories such as those of Tiresias and Cupid often incorporate animals to illustrate timeless and universal messages to warn humans of the dangers of humanity's ongoing battle to control their emotions and overcome animalistic inclinations. Humans are simply animals that have developed a novel type of social structure. To obey the rules that allow the social structure to improve everyone's quality of life, humans must overcome some of their instinctive, animal impulses, habits, and routines. They need the ability to self-regulate in order to do this. Mythology may help people regulate themselves.

The breadth and scope of the natural world provides us with a nearly endless well of organisms to learn from and about. Our knowledge of the biological world is so limited; we have just scratched the surface and are making new discoveries all the time, which is precisely what makes biology so endlessly fascinating. We are only just beginning to learn its mysteries. The unfortunate reality facing biologists is that many species are going extinct before they have even been identified, while other species are lost with just the most basic, rudimentary knowledge of their existence.

Science is the foundation from which knowledge grows and flourishes. It is the lifeblood of a healthy, vigorous society and planet. We will fail the planet and humans will ultimately meet their own demise if we reject science. Scientists occasionally get things wrong, but the beauty of science is that your peers ultimately review and validate or invalidate your work, which allows for knowledge to grow and weeds out information that may be flawed, incorrect, or dated.

It often starts with an observation; those early Greek scientists noticed the peculiar behavior of the love darts in garden snails in their homeland, but it was not fully understood until thousands of years later. Scientific knowledge is often built incrementally. How do we learn and grow as humans? I think all roads lead back to science. Love of science is a gift accessible to all. Let's embrace science before it is too late.

## TWELVE
# NOBLESSE OBLIGE

*"It little profits that an idle king,*
*By this still hearth, among these barren crags,*
*Match'd with an aged wife, I mete and dole*
*Unequal laws unto a savage race,*
*That hoard, and sleep, and feed, and know not me.*
*I cannot rest from travel: I will drink*
*Life to the lees: All times I have enjoy'd*
*Greatly, have suffer'd greatly, both with those*
*That loved me, and alone, on shore, and when*
*Thro' scudding drifts the rainy Hyades*
*Vext the dim sea: I am become a name;*
*For always roaming with a hungry heart*
*Much have I seen and known; cities of men*

And manners, climates, councils, governments,
Myself not least, but honour'd of them all;
And drunk delight of battle with my peers,
Far on the ringing plains of windy Troy.
I am a part of all that I have met;
Yet all experience is an arch wherethro'
Gleams that untravell'd world whose margin fades
For ever and forever when I move.
How dull it is to pause, to make an end,
To rust unburnish'd, not to shine in use!
As tho' to breathe were life! Life piled on life
Were all too little, and of one to me
Little remains: but every hour is saved
From that eternal silence, something more,
A bringer of new things; and vile it were
For some three suns to store and hoard myself,
And this gray spirit yearning in desire
To follow knowledge like a sinking star,
Beyond the utmost bound of human thought.
This is my son, mine own Telemachus,
To whom I leave the sceptre and the isle,—
Well-loved of me, discerning to fulfil
This labour, by slow prudence to make mild
A rugged people, and thro' soft degrees
Subdue them to the useful and the good.
Most blameless is he, centred in the sphere
Of common duties, decent not to fail

*In offices of tenderness, and pay*
*Meet adoration to my household gods,*
*When I am gone. He works his work, I mine.*
*There lies the port; the vessel puffs her sail:*
*There gloom the dark, broad seas. My mariners,*
*Souls that have toil'd, and wrought, and thought with me—*
*That ever with a frolic welcome took*
*The thunder and the sunshine, and opposed*
*Free hearts, free foreheads—you and I are old;*
*Old age hath yet his honour and his toil;*
*Death closes all: but something ere the end,*
*Some work of noble note, may yet be done,*
*Not unbecoming men that strove with Gods.*
*The lights begin to twinkle from the rocks:*
*The long day wanes: the slow moon climbs: the deep*
*Moans round with many voices. Come, my friends,*
*'T is not too late to seek a newer world.*
*Push off, and sitting well in order smite*
*The sounding furrows; for my purpose holds*
*To sail beyond the sunset, and the baths*
*Of all the western stars, until I die.*
*It may be that the gulfs will wash us down:*
*It may be we shall touch the Happy Isles,*
*And see the great Achilles, whom we knew.*
*Tho' much is taken, much abides; and tho'*
*We are not now that strength which in old days*
*Moved earth and heaven, that which we are, we are;*

*One equal temper of heroic hearts,*
*Made weak by time and fate, but strong in will*
*To strive, to seek, to find, and not to yield."*
—ALFRED TENNYSON

## NOBILITY AMONG MEN

*oblesse oblige* is French and literally means "nobility obliges." The phrase was first recorded in France in the 1830s. It is this idea that people who are fortunate enough to be in a high social position either through birth or other means have a moral obligation to act with honor, kindness, and generosity toward those who are less fortunate.

In the book *Burning Daylight*, American author Jack London speaks of noblesse oblige in the following light: "Thus, all unread in philosophy, Daylight preempted for himself the position and vocation of a twentieth-century superman. He found, with rare and mythical exceptions, that there was no noblesse oblige among the business and financial supermen."[80]

Although humans will always struggle with noblesse oblige, there are some mammals that seem to do a better job of it. Gorillas and wolves comprise two of the most iconic images of alpha males in the animal world, falsely associated with violence and aggression when they should be known for their nobility and benevolence.

## GORILLAS

Gorillas are the largest of all the great apes. There are two species of gorillas, the eastern gorilla (*Gorilla beringei*) and the western gorilla (*Gorilla gorilla*). Gorillas are stocky and barrel-chested. They have long arms, short legs, huge heads, and coarse, dark hair. They are exceptionally powerful primates. Males are 1.75 meters in height and weigh on average 180 kilograms, while females are 1.25 meters tall and weigh 100 kilograms. Gorillas exhibit extreme sexual dimorphism, with males being larger than females not only in weight and height but also arm length and strength.

The western (also called lowland) gorilla is found in the forests of equatorial Africa such as Cameroon, Gabon, Equatorial Guinea, Democratic Republic of Congo, and Central African Republic. The eastern gorilla (also called mountain gorilla) inhabits the cloud forest of the Virunga mountains, encompassing the countries of Democratic Republic of Congo, Uganda, and Rwanda. Gorillas primarily feed on leaves but also eat stems, roots, shrubs, fruit, herbs, flowers, and bamboo. They spend roughly 30 percent of their day moving and traveling, 30 percent of the day feeding, and 40 percent resting. Gorillas construct nests out of branches and leaves, usually on the ground, for resting and sleeping.

Gorilla reproduction is very similar to human reproduction. They breed year round. Females menstruate every twenty-eight to thirty days, and gestation is nine months. Gorillas nurse their young for three to four years. Females mature at ten to twelve years and have four-year interbirth intervals. Male gorillas take longer to mature, around eleven to thirteen years old, but they rarely breed before the age of fifteen. As with humans, gorilla infants are very vulnerable and dependent on their mothers for their survival. Mothers provide their babies with food from nursing, transportation via carrying them from place to place, and socialization within the family social unit—they play with them, teach them, and groom them.

Female gorillas provide almost all of the parental care in this species. The role of the parental male is to provide protection for the females and their young from rival troops and the potentially infanticidal alpha-male leader.

Next to the male lion, the male gorilla is one of the most iconic images in the natural world. The males of these species inspire awe, admiration, fear, and horror. They represent sheer strength and power, courage, kings, alphas, and leaders. It is hard not to be impressed by these massive, powerful males.

Mature male gorillas are known as silverbacks for the gray/silver hair found on their backs. Silverbacks dwarf the females and the younger black-backed males in the group, and all of the members of the group defer to them.

In addition to his size and strength, a silverback gorilla also possesses large, sharp canine teeth. A simple glance, frown, or grunt is usually all it takes for him to keep all members of the group in line. He leads and decides where the group travels, where they eat, and where they sleep. When special opportunities arise, like when they come upon a salt lick or a fruiting tree, he determines the amount of time each gorilla gets with the resource. The silverback also serves as the arbitrator between the females in his group. He defends his females and his children from rival males and humans. He is a benevolent leader.

A gorilla group can range in size from two to twenty animals. A gorilla troop consists of one adult silverback (the alpha male) who is usually more than twelve years of age, one black-back male who is usually between eight and eleven years old, three adult females, and the females' children. Adolescent females leave the troop when they are approximately eight years old and join other breeding groups. Often, a female will transfer to a lone silverback just establishing a troop of his own so that she achieves a high rank within the group, which in turn confers extra protection and preferential treatment from the silverback male.

A troop will disband if it loses its alpha male or all of its adult females are lost.

Male gorillas also emigrate. A maturing young adult male emigrates by first staying on the periphery of his soon-to-be-former troop. He stays on the periphery for up to nine months before moving farther away and becoming a solitary silverback male. During his time alone, the silverback becomes more mature and experienced, and by the age of fifteen, he is ready to begin his own harem. The young silverback needs to establish a home range and gain the confidence to successfully lead and defend females and young of his own.

Gorillas, by and large, are placid, amiable animals, with the gentle-giant leader at the center of his troop. Their daily activities include eating, resting, playing, socializing, and making beds. Gorillas remain in this peaceful, shy state unless they are threatened.

The only things that are able to threaten gorillas are rival males, humans, and occasionally a leopard. When gorillas are threatened, the silverback will stand and beat his chest with his fists. They will also growl and aggressively charge toward the intruder, either rushing past or stopping short. Only very rarely does physical hitting occur. Displaying males also give off a pungent odor when they are stressed. This powerful scent is used in chemical communication and can be detected by humans from some distance away. The odor is emitted from their armpits, similar to humans.

Vocal communication is almost entirely done by adult male gorillas. Over 90 percent of all vocalizations are produced by adult males, while females only emit 4 percent of vocalizations. Males utilize a variety of vocalizations depending on the situation. They roar when they are stressed or under threat and usually follow with an aggressive display. Males hoot in conjunction with chest-beating to keep the troop spacing in order and when they see or hear non-group members. Some additional alarm calls include screams, barks, cries, and chuckles. Males also use belches and pig grunts as group-cohesion calls and panting during copulation.

Gorillas also use visual cues, like strutting and facial expressions, to communicate. Some of their facial expressions are shared with humans, including staring, scowling, frowning, pouting, grimacing, and smiling. These confer the same things in both humans and gorillas.

When it comes to reproduction, females are the initiators, approaching the silverback slowly and hesitantly. As the female gets closer, she faces him, with her body slightly turned sideways, waiting for the male to mount her. If he is ready, he will grab her, and she will turn and back into him so he can mount her from behind. Gorillas also copulate belly to belly, but this is not as common.

Gorillas are remarkably like us, from the way they communicate to the odors they produce to their reproduction to their very genes. Gorillas even have individual fingerprints like humans.

The dominant silverback that oversees the group's daily movements and activities, maintains the group's cohesion, and guards the group from outside invaders is the leader of the mountain gorillas' social group. Silverbacks act as role models for young gorillas, teaching them how to build their sleeping nests and what foods to eat. They also educate young males on how to fight and even willingly serve as playmates or as passive climbing frameworks for exuberant infants.

The silverback is a noble creature, showing strength and courage to protect the group from other males and predators. He keeps the group together using intelligence, leadership, and decision-making skills. When teaching youngsters, he exhibits patience, respect, kindness, and gentleness. When the silverback directs daily movements, he uses wisdom, watchfulness, and confidence.

## GRAY WOLVES

The gray wolf (*Canis lupus*) is also an iconic, misunderstood animal. As Canadian writer Farley Mowat stated, "We have doomed the wolf not for what it is, but for what we deliberately and mistakenly perceive it to be—the mythologized epitome of a savage ruthless killer—which is, in reality, no more than a reflected image of ourself."[81] The gray wolf once ranged from the Arctic all the way to Mexico and parts of northern Africa and Asia, but it has been expatriated from most of its original range and now is only found in small areas of the United States, Canada, and Eurasia. Gray wolves inhabit a variety of ecosystems, from forest to tundra and taiga.

Gray wolves are the largest species within the family Canidae. They are powerfully built animals, with large heavy heads and strong jaws and necks, making them efficient predators. Male wolves range in length from 100–160 centimeters, with females averaging 20 centimeters shorter. Males can weigh from 30 to 80 kilograms, while females can weigh from 23 to 55 kilograms. Just as their physical size varies geographically, so does their coloring. The fur color of gray wolves ranges from a mixture of white to gray to brown and black.

Gray wolves are carnivores and prey upon a wide variety of organisms. They hunt in packs for larger prey such as bison, muskoxen, elk, moose, and reindeer. They also engage in solitary hunts for smaller prey such as beavers, rodents, rabbits, and waterfowl. Gray wolves are opportunistic hunters and also eat lizards, snakes, frogs, and insects, as well as stealing the prey of other predators and scavenging carrion. The coastal wolves of British Columbia hunt for salmon, and in the summer months, gray wolves eat berries and melons too. Wolves also hunt livestock and garbage when wild prey becomes scarce.

The dominant male and female in a wolf pack are monogamous. They breed between the months of January and April. Female gray wolves come into estrus only once during a calendar year for five to fourteen days. After mating, the female digs a den to raise her young. She usually selects an area under a cliff or fallen tree or sometimes a cave. The gestation period is around two months, and the litters are usually six or seven pups, but can be as many as fourteen or as few as one. The pups are born in the den and stay there for several weeks after birth. After they're weaned, the pups are fed regurgitated food by members of the pack.

Pups mature quickly, so they can hunt with the pack at ten months old. Females mature quicker than males, reaching full maturity at two years of age, while males do not become fully mature until they are three years old. Most of the young gray wolves leave their natal pack just prior to becoming a mature adult. Gray wolves generally only live five to six years in the wild but can live up to thirteen years.

I think people associate the word *alpha* with wolves. The alpha wolf, the leader of the pack, the alpha dog. This idea that one alpha male wolf is the leader of an enormous pack of wolves is an erroneous one perpetuated by observations of captive populations of wolves.

Scientist L. David Mech was one of the first people to dispel these notions. He discovered that there is an alpha male and alpha female breeding pair at the top of the social order for their particular family.[82] In the wild, a wolf pack usually consists of a breeding pair and their offspring and may include several other families. In captivity, a disparate group of wolves are just thrown together, and in this scenario, they form dominance hierarchies. A wolf pack is simply a family of wolves.

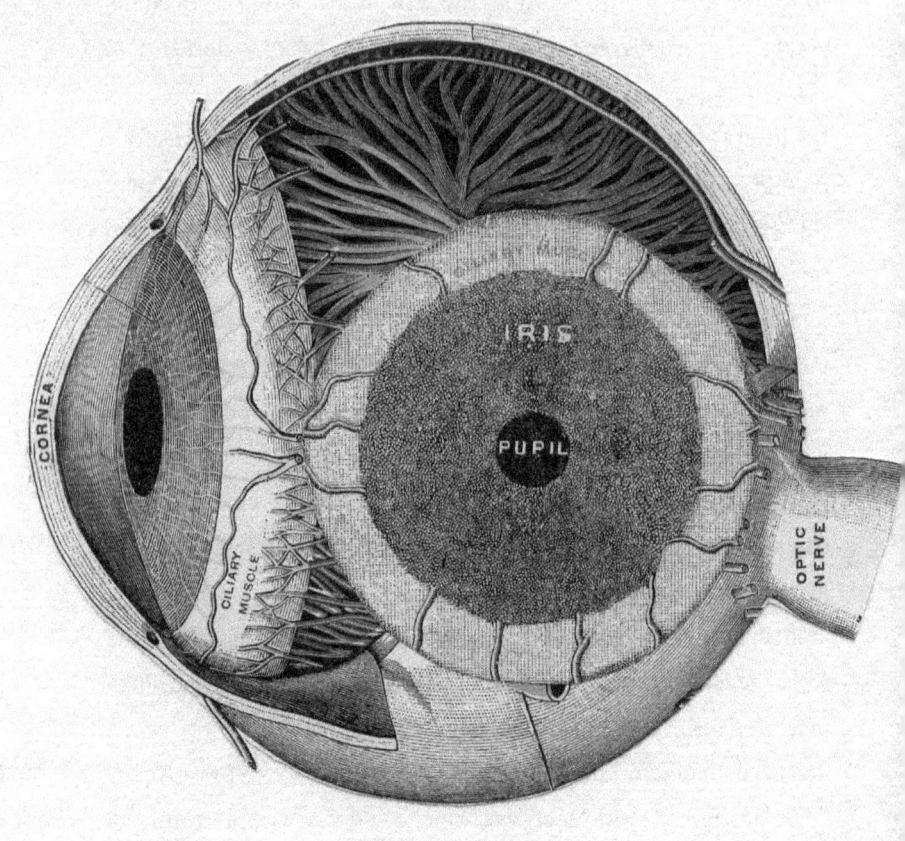

Gray wolves communicate with one another in a variety of ways, including body language, facial expressions, scent marking, and vocalizations. Dominance rank is exhibited through body language and facial expressions. When a more dominant wolf approaches a lower-ranking wolf, the lower-ranking animal licks up toward the dominant animal from a submissive posture.

Another rank interaction involves a dominant wolf standing over a submissive wolf, who lies down and sometimes sniffs the genitals of the higher-ranking animal. An additional pecking order variant in packs occurs when a dominant wolf assumes a standing posture with the tail erect or horizontal while the subordinate animal lowers its body and expresses a cringe facial expression.

Both the alpha male and alpha female scent mark, as do breeding males and breeding females. Subordinate wolves do not scent mark unless they are trying to climb up the dominance hierarchy.

Dominance hierarchies also present themselves regarding food. If a large prey animal has been killed, the pack all eats simultaneously, but if the prey is smaller, the dominant pair determines who eats first. Food allotment is also determined by the alpha wolf.

In the breeding pair, the female is subordinate to the male. The female approaches the male in a subordinate, submissive posture. The only time that this dominance interaction changes is when the breeding female has pups in the den; at this time, the breeding female is temporarily dominant to the breeding male. There is a distinct division of labor between the breeding pair. The female stays around the den area and nurses the pups, while the male hunts and brings back food to the den for the female and the pups.

In gray wolves, the word *alpha* simply refers to the breeding male and the breeding female, who achieved this position simply by mating and producing offspring. This subsequent family unit then becomes a pack. The adult male parent and the adult female parent are considered the dominant breeders or alphas, while a breeding daughter is considered a subordinate breeder. However, most young females leave their birth packs to start their own packs. As L.D. Mech succinctly stated, "The typical wolf pack, then, should be viewed as a family with the adult parents guiding the activities of the group and sharing group leadership in a division-of-labor system in which the female predominates primarily in such activities as pup care and defense and the male primarily during foraging and food-provisioning and the travels associated with them."[83] Does this family life sound familiar to some human families you know?

Wolves are embedded in human culture, folklore, religion, and mythology. They strike fear into the hearts of humans but are also the subject of fascination, scorn, and interest. Wolves appear in the mythology of the Romans, Greeks, Chinese, Hindus, Buddhists, Norse, Pawnee, and Navajo. "Man's best friend" is a descendant of an ancestral wolf from some 20,000 years ago. We may call someone a "lone wolf" and an "old wolf," both with negative and positive connotations.

In many ways, wolves inhabit the subconscious of the human mind. Wolves are thought of both negatively and positively: fear, light, war, cruelty, mistrust, night, protection, destruction, punishment, love, nobility, deceit, danger, cooperation, villainy, curiosity, awe. The wolf resides in a part of our minds that presents the duality of human nature: the ugliness and viciousness, but also the nobility, cooperation, independence, and freedom. The wolves that appear in our fables and literature contribute to the wolf's negative reputation; one needs to look no further than two famous stories, *The Boy Who Cried Wolf* and *Little Red Riding Hood*.

Wolves are complicated, intellectual creatures that value family above all else. They are playful, compassionate, complex, and noble creatures. Wolves raise their young, tend to their injured, and live in family groups. Individual wolves also show each other attention. They care for their injured and ill. Pack structure facilitates intergenerational knowledge transfer and communication. Wolves possess and transmit what is most accurately referred to as culture. A family unit can last for several generations, perhaps for decades, passing down wisdom and information from one generation to the next. Wolves work across generations, communicate, and exchange knowledge. The older wolves, who are more skilled hunters, impart their expertise to the younger wolves, passing it down from one generation to the next and preserving the particular culture of that pack.

## ELEPHANTS

What creature is more noble than the elephant? Adults and children alike have a look of awe, amazement and joy when they look at elephants. Elephants command our respect and admiration.

Elephants are the largest land animals on the planet. Of the three elephant species, the African bush elephant (*Loxodonta africana*) is the largest. Male bush elephants can reach a shoulder height of 4 meters, while females can reach 3.4 meters. Males can weigh up to an astounding 6,300 kilograms and females 3,500 kilograms. Elephants are unmistakable with their trunks, tusks, and big ears. They have thick, gray skin with short, coarse bristles on their trunks and chins. They use their massive ears not only to hear but also to communicate with other elephants and to fan themselves, cooling them down in the hot sun. They use their muscular trunks, which are a combination of a nose and an upper lip, to move and grab things, smell, touch, make sounds, and breathe. Both male and female elephants have tusks, which are modified incisor teeth. Elephants use their tusks for a variety of tasks such as fighting, defending, digging, moving items, and marking trees.

African bush elephants have a patchy distribution below the Sahara and are found in countries such as Kenya, Tanzania, Botswana, Zambia, South Africa, and Gabon. Bush elephants inhabit a variety of ecosystems such as scrub forests, grasslands, savannas, and woodlands. Elephants feed on woody plants in the dry season and grasses and herbs in the lush rainy season. Their feeding habits can change ecosystems; they have been known to change woodlands into grasslands.

The social organization of the African bush elephant centers around the herd matriarch. The herd consists of the matriarch (the mother), her daughters, and their young. These social units range in size from two to twenty-four elephants, with the most common size being around nine to eleven individuals. The group stays close together, with the matriarch determining everything: where and when to feed, when to rest, and in what direction they will move. The leadership experience of the matriarch is of paramount importance to the herd. Without her, the herd struggles mightily.

Elephants do not abandon injured herd members; instead, they try to lift and comfort them. They also mourn their dead.

Male elephants form their own herds. Once male elephants reach adolescence, they leave the maternal herd. Some males go at it alone, while others form bachelor herds. Typically, younger males associate with other immature males, while bachelor herds consist of males of a wide age range.

African bush elephants communicate in a variety of ways, including vocalizations, touch, and smells. Elephants utilize four different sounds to communicate, but much like humans, the volume, duration, and pitch of those sounds can communicate a myriad of emotions. Rumbling is a vocalization thought to be used over great distances, conferring social and sexual status to allow for the meeting or avoiding of other elephants. These rumblings often occur at frequencies undetectable by human hearing. Growling is a form of rumbling that is used when greeting another elephant. A growl can also turn into a roar when an elephant is threatening predators. A bellow is used when an elephant experiences pain or fear. Trumpeting is a sound created through the trunk; it signals excitement and is used to sound the alarm to other members in the herd or to cry for help. This type of vocalization is also used during greeting ceremonies. Juveniles squeal when they are under distress, which elicits an immediate response from the mother. Adults scream when they are trying to intimidate rival elephants.

Anyone who has seen elephants interact knows that they are physical animals. They constantly touch and rub against one another. During a greeting ceremony, the lower-ranking elephant inserts their trunk into the mouth of the other elephant. Calves exhibit a similar behavior with their mothers for reassurance or to sample food. Mothers often guide or steer their offspring by gripping their tails. Fighting elephants will sometimes wrestle with their trunks, and courting elephants will often intertwine their trunks.

Elephants have an array of dominance and threat displays as well as defensive or submissive displays that they use both within their herds and when coming into contact with other herds. Standing tall is a dominance display, with the head held high and ears alert but back.

A front-trunk swish is a threat display that is usually accompanied by trumpeting. Threat displays are used to issue challenges, commonly preceding fights among younger male elephants. These fights teach young elephants lessons about their own strength and where they fall within the hierarchy as they grow. African bush elephants grow larger throughout their lifetimes, unlike humans, who stop growing at the end of adolescence.

An elephant's size is correlational to dominance, which is predicated on age or seniority. When two bull elephants meet and one is obviously smaller in size, the smaller male lowers his head, flattens his ears, and moves backward while making writhing trunk movements. The larger male follows, and once he makes contact, the deferring male puts his trunk in the dominant male's mouth in the traditional greeting manner. The dominant male asserts his position in the hierarchy by holding his head high, trunk hanging and ears somewhat spread.

When two bulls of roughly equal size approach one another, they measure each other up by coming together with their heads raised until their trunks and tusks are touching. Once the trunks and tusks are engaged, they begin pushing and fighting. Usually the larger, more confident male wins these confrontations. Violent fights involving ramming and goring are rare.

Female elephants allow males to approach and check their reproductive status. This is done by the male putting the tip of his trunk into the female's genital opening and then into his mouth. The scent or secretions of the female signal when she is most fertile.

The courtship phase involves a male approaching a female and attempting to stroke her with his trunk. Often the female will retreat when pursued by a bull. When the female stops retreating, she reciprocates the trunk-stroking with the male. The courtship continues with the female presenting her hindquarters to the male. The male then rests his chin and tusks on her backside and mounts the female.

Musth is a condition found in male elephants that is characterized by secretions from the temporal glands, continuous discharge of urine, increased aggressive behavior, and elevated levels of testosterone. Unlike a rut, common in other mammals, musth does not occur synchronously among adult males. Musth enhances a male's ability to approach reproductively active females through increasing mobility and elevating dominance via intrasexual competition but is energetically costly, as musth males range more widely than non-musth males.

Research scientist Julie Hollister-Smith determined that female elephants prefer older musth males as mates. Two reproductive strategies emerge in African elephants: musth and sexually active non-musth. Therefore, it may be strategically advantageous for a particular male to use a non-musth strategy, in which the male remains out of musth in order to avoid musth-male attention while still attempting to mate with suitable estrous females. Strategies change depending on the size of the male. Scientist Joyce Poole has found that musth strategy involves balancing costs and advantages rather than just remaining in musth for as long as is physiologically possible, at least for small and medium-sized males.[84] The smaller the male, the less time he spends in musth because it is a less viable mating strategy. Poole's research has also revealed that in cases where the available estrous females are already monopolized by a high-ranking male, low-ranking males are more likely to secure a copulation when they are not in musth and when they are not guarding females.

## CONCLUSION

Each of the previous examples shows a majestic animal—noble, even. However, more than merely their impressive stature, these animals are an inspiration when we consider the complex mechanisms of their social structures. The conceptual sophistication of *noblesse oblige* would like us to believe that privilege explicitly imposes a commitment on those who enjoy privilege to those who have less. And surely these animals demonstrate a complex structure to ensure that they protect their own (even *from* their own) in a social structure that is not necessarily altruistic but robust and seemingly self-aware.

We like to believe that modern society is civilized, educated, evolved—that we no longer engage in the brutal aggression and sexual politics embodied in the animal world. There is a double layer of complexity in this when we turn that lens to the astonishing beauty of the gorilla, the wolf, and the elephant. Does our reverence and awe of these animals make them noble? Surely they are astonishing. But what is it about nobility that resides so deeply within our collective psyche that they are both loathed and admired—even emulated? Certainly, they stir our souls, conjuring images of social, sexual, and violent dominance. They make us question our place in society. They inspire awe and admiration but sometimes also fear. Whatever they do, they stand out from the crowd, leaving an indelible impression on those whose lives they touch.

# CONCLUSION

"Whales in mid-ocean, suspended in the waves of the sea great heaven of whales in the waters, old hierarchies. And enormous mother whales lie dreaming suckling their whale-tender young and dreaming with strange whale eyes wide open in the water of the beginning and the end."

—DAVID HERBERT LAWRENCE

## SOCIAL MAMMALS

Humans are social mammals with large brains; we organize ourselves in hierarchies that influence access to power, sex, and status. Ideally, hierarchical structures should be benign—and in many cases they are. But they can also be abused.

We humans organize ourselves into a wide variety of social groups. We are tribal creatures with strong familial ties. We are violent and deceitful but also peaceful, honest, and noble. We really are an odd organism. We have this incredibly large, magnificent brain that allows us to live (or makes us believe that we can live) almost on a parallel track to the rest of the biomass of the planet. Some of us want to view ourselves as greater than, following instead a path that is divergent, tangential, ascending above. I think the beauty lies in the intersecting points, the commonalities between *Homo sapiens* and our plant and animal brethren. The more we learn from and respect life on earth, the better we will become as a species—and, as a result, the more integrated with the global whole.

Love is a universal experience. We've seen that all through the animal kingdom, and we know it from our experiences as humans. You could view this book as my love letter to science—to biology specifically.

## STUDY OF LIFE

Biology, quite simply, is the study of life. Scientists throughout the ages, from well before Aristotle to E.O. Wilson, have studied life on earth. By studying other living organisms, we can unlock information that helps us not only in a practical sense but also in indirect ways to make sense of the world. I am infinitely interested in life on earth, and I am excited and horrified by how little we actually know about other organisms that inhabit the planet with us. For my love of the unknown, filling in the blank spaces through biology and exploration, field work, lab work, building from previous research, or creating new pathways for discovery and knowledge is incredibly fulfilling.

We generally think of love as a uniquely human experience, but I think we can safely ascribe it to other mammalian species as well. Anthropologist Helen Fisher has identified three stages of love: lust (the early, intense sexual urge that encourages mating), attraction (the more individualized yearning for a particular mating prospect), and attachment (the bonding that encourages long-lasting relationships). These three stages are found in a variety of species.

What is the result of this drive for love in the animal world? As we saw in Part 1 of this book, it has created highly specialized senses. Our sense of sight is highly attuned to recognizing specific body shapes and sizes when selecting partners, while some lizards and birds use colors to communicate status. An organism's sense of hearing plays an important role in many aspects of life, especially when it comes to finding partners and communicating with individuals with different levels of status. Sounds made by prospective mates are important in bats and crickets, but being the loudest is not always best, as we learned with bison. Human voice pitch is an interesting variable used in social settings, not only in mate selection but also in altering one's own voice depending on a person's position of power within a social hierarchy.

Smell is another sense used quite frequently in the animal kingdom. Chemical scents communicate a variety of things within a species. In lemmings and mice, females can determine winners and losers from previous fights just by smelling the males. Humans use scents to communicate their genetic fitness to the opposite sex.

The quest for power, status, and sex is illustrated in Part 2 by Genghis Khan, Moulay Ismail Ibn Sharif, and Charlemagne. It has spurred the construction of complex social hierarchies and triggered wars. These men represent the spoils of pursuing power, sex, and status in unrelenting ways but also the ugliness of human nature. Humans are not the only primate that resorts to violence to move up or maintain power within a hierarchy; macaques, baboons, and chimpanzees all follow suit. Female-dominant species such as pipefish, hyenas, and honeybees show a different social structure that is not dependent on violence to succeed.

Part 3 explored the significance of arenas for humans but also birds such as prairie chickens, grouse, and marine iguanas. A male's location within the arena communicates information to the females observing the contests. Ultimately, the females decide whom they are going to mate with depending on the information that they collect from the arena encounters. As we also saw in this part, some organisms have evolved to have weaponry. Bighorn sheep, rusty crayfish, and horned beetles all use weapons to fight other males and fend off rivals. Individuals that are not as adept at fighting have developed different strategies to gain reproductive opportunities. The evolutionary arms race has also spurred or forced underdogs to develop covert strategies to succeed. Humans, bluegills, and red deer all have employed sneaky courtship maneuvers to create mating opportunities for themselves.

One of the strongest and quickest evolutionary processes is

sexual selection, or competition between individuals of one sex for reproductive access to individuals of the other. It has nurtured conventional and nonconventional marriages, and it has even enabled some species to change their sex or to have both male and female reproductive organs in one individual.

Polygyny is common in many communities around the world. Polygyny is also found in elephant seals, lions, and horses, among many other species as well. Blue-headed wrasses are able to change their sex, and flatworms and snails are hermaphrodites. All of these species highlight the breadth and scope of the different approaches to reproduction via sexual selection.

## HIERARCHIES

Hierarchies in nonhuman species are typically formed over time by means of repeated threats and fighting. Once order has been established, few hostile exchanges occur. In the animal kingdom, ranking high in the social hierarchy assures access to necessities like food and to privileges such as mating opportunities. Individuals often move up and down the ranks, and an alpha's position at the top can be short-lived. Low-ranking males learn from the dominants and occasionally challenge top-ranking males. Subordinates emigrate to other social groups, adapt to dominants, and sneak copulations with estrous females. In some cases, subordinates simply wait for dominant animals to grow old and die. Human males and females are unique in their flexibility to use combinations of many strategies.

Studies have shown that across cultures, human males and females look for the same set of qualities in each other, such as attractiveness, intelligence, kindness, physical fitness, and access to economic resources. It is very rare that any male or female has the full complement of qualities, and therefore the respective parties must settle for individuals that have some of the aforementioned qualities.

Although hierarchy is a fundamental organizing concept in biology and a major factor in how evolution develops sophisticated, adaptable species, little is known about its origins. As we have seen throughout this book, in many species, social groupings quickly self-organize into hierarchies, with members varying in their degree of dominance, skill, influence, and power.

Early on in life, we are taught to think of our social environment in terms of who is better, wiser, or more popular than everyone else. I remember very distinctly competing in sports such as soccer and basketball, worrying about standardized test scores and grade point averages, and recognizing who was popular and who was not popular in school. Even as adults, we are able to quickly recognize status markers like expensive automobiles, large homes, and professional titles. The way we interpret social cues and rank people reflects our general predilection for hierarchical social structures. Maybe because establishing social roles and encouraging fruitful social engagement depend on knowing where we stand in relation to others. Social hierarchies are endemic and intrinsic, and they most likely evolved to assist survival in a context of group existence.

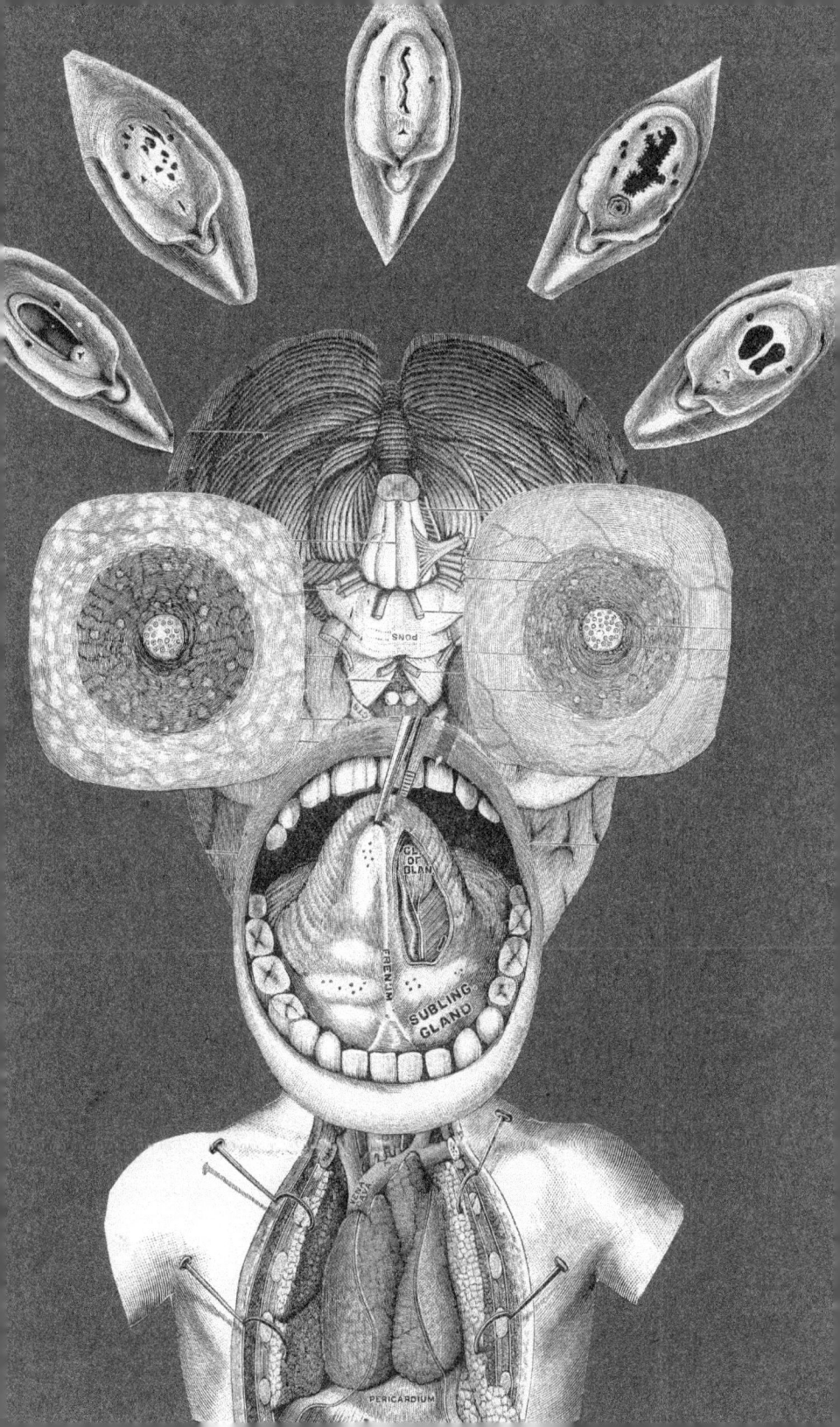

Power, status, and sex are a fascinating and complex set of topics that we have covered throughout this book, looking at a variety of examples from the animal kingdom. These things do not stay static; they are always changing and evolving. They are highly flexible and often incredibly complex, especially as applied to humans. New research will continue to emerge that will further our understanding of power, status, and sex in the natural world.

# NOTES

1 Leivers, Samantha, Leigh W. Simmons, and Gillian Rhodes. "Men's sexual faithfulness judgments may contain a kernel of truth." *PloS One* 10.8 (2015): e0134007.
2 Rhodes, Gillian, Grace Morley, and Leigh W. Simmons. "Women can judge sexual unfaithfulness from unfamiliar men's faces." *Biology letters* 9.1 (2013): 20120908.
3 Schmitt, David P., and David M. Buss. "Human mate poaching: Tactics and temptations for infiltrating existing mateships." *Journal of personality and Social Psychology* 80.6 (2001): 894.
4 Sinervo, Barry, and Curt M. Lively. "The rock–paper–scissors game and the evolution of alternative male strategies." *Nature* 380.6571 (1996): 240-243.
5 Franklin, Donald C. and P. L. Dostine. "A note on the frequency and genetics of head colour morphs in the Gouldian finch." *Emu-Austral Ornithology* 100.3 (2000): 236-239.
6 Dixson, Alan F., et al. "Masculine somatotype and hirsuteness as determinants of sexual attractiveness to women." *Archives of Sexual Behavior* 32 (2003): 29-39.

7   Singh, D., Dixson, B. J., Jessop, T. S., Morgan, B., & Dixson, A. F. (2010). "Cross-cultural consensus for waist–hip ratio and women's attractiveness." *Evolution and Human Behavior*, 31(3): 176-181.
8   Pierce, C. A. (1996). "Body height and romantic attraction: A meta-analytic test of the male-taller norm." *Social Behavior and Personality: an International Journal* 24(2): 143-149.
9   Stulp, Gert, Abraham P. Buunk, and Thomas V. Pollet. "Women want taller men more than men want shorter women." *Personality and Individual Differences* 54.8 (2013): 877-883.
10  Stulp, G., Pollet, T. V., Verhulst, S., & Buunk, A. P. (2012). "A curvilinear effect of height on reproductive success in human males." *Behavioral Ecology and Sociobiology* 66: 375-384.
11  Dixson, Alan F. *Sexual selection and the origins of human mating systems.* Oxford University Press, 2009.
12  Scheib, Joanna E. "Context-specific mate choice criteria: Women's trade-offs in the contexts of long-term and extra-pair mateships." *Personal Relationships* 8, no. 4 (2001): 371-389.
13  Sinervo, Barry, and Curt M. Lively. "The rock–paper–scissors game and the evolution of alternative male strategies." *Nature* 380.6571 (1996): 240-243.
14  Re, Daniel E., Jillian JM O'Connor, Patrick J. Bennett, and David R. Feinberg. "Preferences for very low and very high voice pitch in humans." *PloS One* 7, no. 3 (2012): e32719.
15  Puts, David Andrew, Steven JC Gaulin, and Katherine Verdolini. "Dominance and the evolution of sexual dimorphism in human voice pitch." *Evolution and Human Behavior* 27.4 (2006): 283-296.
16  Anderson, Rindy C., and Casey A. Klofstad. "Preference for leaders with masculine voices holds in the case of feminine leadership roles." *PloS One* 7, no. 12 (2012): e51216.
17  Gray, David A. "Female house crickets, Acheta domesticus, prefer the chirps of large males." *Animal Behaviour* 54.6 (1997): 1553-1562.
18  Crankshaw, Owen S. "Female choice in relation to calling and courtship songs in Acheta domesticus." *Animal Behaviour* 27 (1979): 1274-1275.
19  Wyman, Megan T., et al. "Amplitude of bison bellows reflects male quality, physical condition and motivation." *Animal Behaviour* 76.5 (2008): 1625-1639.

20  Voigt, Christian C., et al. "Songs, scents, and senses: sexual selection in the greater sac-winged bat, Saccopteryx bilineata." *Journal of Mammalogy* 89.6 (2008): 1401-1410.
21  Puts, David Andrew, et al. "Men's voices as dominance signals: vocal fundamental and formant frequencies influence dominance attributions among men." *Evolution and Human Behavior* 28.5 (2007): 340-344.
22  Puts, David Andrew. "Mating context and menstrual phase affect women's preferences for male voice pitch." *Evolution and Human Behavior* 26, no. 5 (2005): 388-397.
23  Hodges-Simeon, Carolyn R., Steven JC Gaulin, and David A. Puts. "Voice correlates of mating success in men: examining 'contests' versus 'mate choice' modes of sexual selection." *Archives of Sexual Behavior* 40 (2011): 551-557.
24  Fraccaro, P. J., Jones, B. C., Vukovic, J., Smith, F. G., Watkins, C. D., Feinberg, D. R., ... & Debruine, L. M. (2011). "Experimental evidence that women speak in a higher voice pitch to men they find attractive." *Journal of Evolutionary Psychology* 9(1): 57-67.
25  Apicella, Coren L., David R. Feinberg, and Frank W. Marlowe. "Voice pitch predicts reproductive success in male hunter-gatherers." *Biology Letters* 3, no. 6 (2007): 682-684.
26  Evans, Sarah, Nick Neave, and Delia Wakelin. "Relationships between vocal characteristics and body size and shape in human males: an evolutionary explanation for a deep male voice." *Biological Psychology* 72.2 (2006): 160-163.
27  Valentova, J. V., Tureček, P., Varella, M. A. C., Šebesta, P., Mendes, F. D. C., Pereira, K. J., ... & Havlíček, J. (2019). "Vocal parameters of speech and singing covary and are related to vocal attractiveness, body measures, and sociosexuality: a cross-cultural study." *Frontiers in Psychology* 10: 2029.
28  Wedekind, Claus, et al. "MHC-dependent mate preferences in humans." *Proceedings of the Royal Society of London. Series B: Biological Sciences* 260.1359 (1995): 245-249.
29  Grammer, Karl, Bernhard Fink, and Nick Neave. "Human pheromones and sexual attraction." *European Journal of Obstetrics & Gynecology and Reproductive Biology* 118.2 (2005): 135-142.

30  Ebster, Claus, and Michael Kirk-Smith. "The effect of the human pheromone androstenol on product evaluation." *Psychology & Marketing* 22.9 (2005): 739-749.

31  Huoviala, Paavo, and Markus J. Rantala. "A putative human pheromone, androstadienone, increases cooperation between men." *PLoS One* 8.5 (2013): e62499.

32  Huck, U. William, and Edwin M. Banks. "Differential attraction of females to dominant males: olfactory discrimination and mating preference in the brown lemming (Lemmus trimucronatus)." *Behavioral Ecology and Sociobiology* 11 (1982): 217-222.

33  Flood, P. F., Abrams, S. R., Muir, G. D., & Rowell, J. E. (1989). "Odor of the muskox: a preliminary investigation." *Journal of Chemical Ecology* 15: 2207-2217.

34  Havlíček, J., Dvořáková, R., Bartoš, L., & Flegr, J. (2006). "Non-advertized does not mean concealed: body odour changes across the human menstrual cycle." *Ethology* 112(1): 81-90.

35  Buss, David M., and Todd K. Shackelford. "Attractive women want it all: Good genes, economic investment, parenting proclivities, and emotional commitment." *Evolutionary Psychology* 6.1 (2008): 147470490800600116.

36  Miller, Saul L., and Jon K. Maner. "Scent of a woman: Men's testosterone responses to olfactory ovulation cues." *Psychological Science* 21.2 (2010): 276-283.

37  Gangestad, Steven W., and Randy Thornhill. "Menstrual cycle variation in women's preferences for the scent of symmetrical men." *Proceedings of the Royal Society of London. Series B: Biological Sciences* 265.1399 (1998): 927-933.

38  Trivers, Robert L. "Parental investment and sexual selection." In *Sexual Selection and the Descent of Man*. Routledge, 2017. 136-179.

39  Thornhill, Randy, and Steven W. Gangestad. "The scent of symmetry: A human sex pheromone that signals fitness?" *Evolution and Human Behavior* 20.3 (1999): 175-201.

40  Williams, Megan N., and Amy Jacobson. "Effect of copulins on rating of female attractiveness, mate-guarding, and self-perceived sexual desirability." *Evolutionary Psychology* 14.2 (2016): 1474704916643328.

41  Lessem, Don. *The Wit and Wisdom of Genghis Khan*. Dino Don, Inc., 2009. 1-40.
42  Zerjal, T., Xue, Y., Bertorelle, G., Wells, R. S., Bao, W., Zhu, S., ... & Tyler-Smith, C. (2003). "The genetic legacy of the Mongols." *The American Journal of Human Genetics* 72(3): 717-721.
43  Oberzaucher, Elisabeth, and Karl Grammer. "The case of Moulay Ismael-fact or fancy?" *PloS One* 9.2 (2014): e85292.
44  Sullivan, Richard Eugene. *Aix-la-Chapelle in the Age of Charlemagne*. No. 10. Norman, U. of Oklahoma P, 1963.
45  Lea, A. J., Akinyi, M. Y., Nyakundi, R., Mareri, P., Nyundo, F., Kariuki, T., ... & Tung, J. (2018). "Dominance rank-associated gene expression is widespread, sex-specific, and a precursor to high social status in wild male baboons." *Proceedings of the National Academy of Sciences* 115(52): E12163-E12171.
46  Gesquiere, L. R., Learn, N. H., Simao, M. C. M., Onyango, P. O., Alberts, S. C., & Altmann, J. (2011). "Life at the top: rank and stress in wild male baboons." *Science* 333(6040): 357-360.
47  Anderson, J. A., Johnston, R. A., Lea, A. J., Campos, F. A., Voyles, T. N., Akinyi, M. Y., ... & Tung, J. (2021). "High social status males experience accelerated epigenetic aging in wild baboons." *Elife* 10, e66128.
48  De Waal, Frans. "The Surprising Science of Alpha Males." TED Video, 2017, 15:44, https://www.ted.com/talks/frans_de_waal_the_surprising_science_of_alpha_males?language=en
49  Bell, Daniel A. and Wang Pei. *Just hierarchy: Why social hierarchies matter in China and the rest of the world*. Princeton University Press, 2020.
50  Berglund, Anders, and Gunilla Rosenqvist. "Male pipefish prefer ornamented females." *Animal Behaviour* 61.2 (2001): 345-350.
51  Monteiro, Nuno, Maria da Natividade Vieira, and Vitor C. Almada. "The courtship behaviour of the pipefish Nerophis lumbriciformis: reflections of an adaptation to intertidal life." *Acta Ethologica* 4 (2002): 109-111.
52  Glickman, S. E., Zabel, C. J., Yoerg, S. I., Weldele, M. L., Drea, C. M., & Frank, L. G. (1997). "Social facilitation, affiliation, and dominance in the social life of spotted hyenas." *Annals of the New York Academy of Sciences-Paper Edition* 807: 175-184.

53  East, Marion L., and Heribert Hofer. "Male spotted hyenas (Crocuta crocuta) queue for status in social groups dominated by females." *Behavioral Ecology* 12.5 (2001): 558-568.
54  Muller, Martin N., and Richard Wrangham. "Sexual mimicry in hyenas." *The Quarterly Review of Biology* 77.1 (2002): 3-16.
55  Sumra, Monika K. "Masculinity, femininity, and leadership: Taking a closer look at the alpha female." *PLoS One* 14.4 (2019): e0215181.
56  Mast, Marianne Schmid. "Female dominance hierarchies: Are they any different from males'?" *Personality and Social Psychology Bulletin* 28.1 (2002): 29-39.
57  Wikelski, Martin, Chris Carbone, and Fritz Trillmich. "Lekking in marine iguanas: female grouping and male reproductive strategies." *Animal Behaviour* 52.3 (1996): 581-596.
58  Boehm, Christopher, and Christopher Boehm. *Hierarchy in the Forest: The Evolution of Egalitarian Behavior*. Harvard University Press, 2009.
59  Bell, Daniel A. and Wang Pei. *Just Hierarchy: Why Social Hierarchies Matter in China and the Rest of the World*. Princeton University Press, 2020.
60  Henrich, Joseph, and Francisco J. Gil-White. "The evolution of prestige: Freely conferred deference as a mechanism for enhancing the benefits of cultural transmission." *Evolution and Human Behavior* 22.3 (2001): 165-196.
61  Pelletier, Fanie, John T. Hogg, and Marco Festa-Bianchet. "Male mating effort in a polygynous ungulate." *Behavioral Ecology and Sociobiology* 60 (2006): 645-654.
62  Hogg, John T., and Stephen H. Forbes. "Mating in bighorn sheep: frequent male reproduction via a high-risk 'unconventional' tactic." *Behavioral Ecology and Sociobiology* 41 (1997): 33-48.
63  Schroeder, Lisa, and Robert Huber. "Fight strategies differ with size and allometric growth of claws in crayfish, Orconectes rusticus." *Behaviour* 138.11-12 (2001): 1437-1449.
64  Emlen, Douglas J. "Alternative reproductive tactics and male-dimorphism in the horned beetle Onthophagus acuminatus (Coleoptera: Scarabaeidae)." *Behavioral Ecology and Sociobiology* 41 (1997): 335-341.

65  Touraille, Priscille and Pierre-Henri Gouyon. "Why are women smaller than men? When anthropology meets evolutionary biology." *Nature Precedings* (2008): 1-1.
66  Fessler, Daniel MT. "No time to eat: An adaptationist account of periovulatory behavioral changes." *The Quarterly Review of Biology* 78.1 (2003): 3-21.
67  Dunsworth, Holly M. "Expanding the evolutionary explanations for sex differences in the human skeleton." *Evolutionary Anthropology: Issues, News, and Reviews* 29.3 (2020): 108-116.
68  Colman, Andrew M. *A Dictionary of Psychology*. Oxford Quick Reference, 2015.
69  Huffard, Christine L., Roy L. Caldwell, and Farnis Boneka. "Mating behavior of Abdopus aculeatus (d'Orbigny 1834)(Cephalopoda: Octopodidae) in the wild." *Marine Biology* 154 (2008): 353-362.
70  Clutton-Brock, Tim H., and Steven D. Albon. "The roaring of red deer and the evolution of honest advertisement." *Behaviour* 69.3-4 (1979): 145-170.
71  Owens, Delia. *Where the Crawdads Sing (Movie Tie-In)*. Penguin, 2022.
72  Buss, David M. *The Evolution of Desire: Strategies of Human Mating*. Hachette UK, 2016.
73  Ahinkorah, Bright Opoku. "Polygyny and intimate partner violence in sub-Saharan Africa: Evidence from 16 cross-sectional demographic and health surveys." *SSM-Population Health* 13 (2021): 100729.
74  Kappeler, Peter M., and Carel P. Van Schaik, eds. *Sexual Selection in Primates: New and Comparative Perspectives*. Cambridge University Press, 2004.
75  Moorad, J. A., Promislow, D. E., Smith, K. R., & Wade, M. J. (2011). "Mating system change reduces the strength of sexual selection in an American frontier population of the 19th century." *Evolution and Human Behavior* 32(2): 147-155.
76  Grice, A. L. "2017 American Horse Council economic impact study." *Proceedings of the 64th Annual Convention of the American Association of Equine Practitioners, San Francisco, California, USA, 1-5 December 2018*. American Association of Equine Practitioners (AAEP), 2018.
77  Michiels, Nicolaas K., and L. J. Newman. "Sex and violence in hermaphrodites." *Nature* 391.6668 (1998): 647-647.

78  Michiels, Nico K., and Blanka Bakovski. "Sperm trading in a hermaphroditic flatworm: reluctant fathers and sexy mothers." *Animal Behaviour* 59.2 (2000): 319-325.
79  Koene, Joris M., and Ronald Chase. "Changes in the reproductive system of the snail Helix aspersa caused by mucus from the love dart." *The Journal of Experimental Biology* 201.15 (1998): 2313-2319.
80  London, Jack. *Burning Daylight*. Macmillan Company, 1910.
81  Mowat, Farley. *Never Cry Wolf*. McClelland & Stewart, 2009.
82  Mech, L. David. "Alpha status, dominance, and division of labor in wolf packs." *Canadian Journal of Zoology* 77.8 (1999): 1196-1203.
83  Mech, L. David. "Alpha status, dominance, and division of labor in wolf packs." *Canadian Journal of Zoology* 77.8 (1999): 1196-1203.
84  Poole, J. H., Lee, P. C., Njiraini, N., & Moss, C. J. (2011). 18. "Longevity, Competition, and Musth: A Long-Term Perspective on Male Reproductive Strategies." In *The Amboseli elephants: A Long-Term Perspective on a Long-Lived Mammal* (pp. 272-288). University of Chicago Press.

# ADDITIONAL REFERENCES

Hill, Russell A., and Robert A. Barton. "Red enhances human performance in contests." *Nature* 435.7040 (2005): 293-293.

Feinberg, D. R., Jones, B. C., Smith, M. L., Moore, F. R., DeBruine, L. M., Cornwell, R. E., ... & Perrett, D. I. (2006). "Menstrual cycle, trait estrogen level, and masculinity preferences in the human voice." *Hormones and behavior* 49(2): 215-222.

Snedden, W. Andy. "Determinants of male mating success in the temperate crayfish Orconectes rusticus: chela size and sperm competition." *Behaviour* 115.1-2 (1990): 100-113.

Emlen, Douglas J. "Environmental control of horn length dimorphism in the beetle Onthophagus acuminatus (Coleoptera: Scarabaeidae)." *Proceedings of the Royal Society of London. Series B: Biological Sciences* 256.1346 (1994): 131-136.

Janfaza, M., Sherman, T. I., Larmore, K. A., Brown-Dawson, J., & Klein, K. O. (2006). "Estradiol levels and secretory dynamics in normal girls and boys as determined by an ultrasensitive bioassay: a 10 year experience." *Journal of Pediatric Endocrinology and Metabolism* 19(7): 901-910.

Landolfa, Michael A., David M. Green, and Ronald Chase. "Dart shooting influences paternal reproductive success in the snail Helix aspersa (Pulmonata, Stylommatophora)." *Behavioral Ecology* 12.6 (2001): 773-777.

Mech, L. David, and Luigi Boitani, eds. *Wolves: behavior, ecology, and conservation.* University of Chicago Press, 2007.

Hollister-Smith, J. A., Poole, J. H., Archie, E. A., Vance, E. A., Georgiadis, N. J., Moss, C. J., & Alberts, S. C. (2007). "Age, musth and paternity success in wild male African elephants, Loxodonta africana." *Animal Behaviour* 74(2): 287-296.

Poole, J. H., Kasman, L. H., Ramsay, E. C., & Lasley, B. L. (1984). "Musth and urinary testosterone concentrations in the African elephant (Loxodonta africana)." *Reproduction* 70(1): 255-260.

Frederick, William H. "History of Southeast Asia". *Encyclopedia Britannica*, 20 Jul. 2018, https://www.britannica.com/topic/history-of-Southeast-Asia-556509. Accessed 30 August 2023.

Maestripieri, Dario. *Macachiavellian intelligence: how rhesus macaques and humans have conquered the world.* University of Chicago Press, 2019.

De Waal, Frans. "The Surprising Science of Alpha Males." TED Video, 2017, 15:44, https://www.ted.com/talks/frans_de_waal_the_surprising_science_of_alpha_males?language=en

Nochlin, Linda."Riot Girl, Black Anna." https://archive.nytimes.com/www.nytimes.com/library/magazine/millennium/m2/irritating-anna.html

www.ingramcontent.com/pod-product-compliance
Lightning Source LLC
Chambersburg PA
CBHW020455030426
42337CB00011B/125